Series Editor: Robert Unwin

The Industrial Revolution

Robert Unwin

Hutchinson

London Melbourne Sydney Auckland Johannesburg

Hutchinson & Co. (Publishers) Ltd

An imprint of the Hutchinson Publishing Group

17-21 Conway Street, London W1P 5HL

Hutchinson Group (Australia) Pty Ltd
30-32 Cremorne Street, Richmond South, Victoria 3121
PO Box 151, Broadway, New South Wales 2007

Hutchinson Group (NZ) Ltd
32-34 View Road, PO Box 40-086, Glenfield, Auckland 10

Hutchinson Group (SA) (Pty) Ltd
PO Box 337, Bergvlei 2012, South Africa

First published 1980
Reprinted 1981
© Robert Unwin 1980

Set in IBM Univers and Century by Tek·art Ltd

Printed in Great Britain by The Anchor Press Ltd
and bound by Wm Brendon & Son Ltd,
both of Tiptree, Essex

British Library Cataloguing in Publication Data

Openings in history
    The Industrial Revolution
    I. Great Britain — History
    I. Unwin, Robert William, b.1938
    II. Industrial Revolution
941   DA32

ISBN 0 09 141291 9

Contents

1 Changes on the farm

2 How many people were working on the farm altogether? Are there any people not employed?

3 Which picture (a or b) shows the earlier scene? Give reasons for your answer.

4 List all the differences you can see between the two pictures.

5 There were many reasons why the changes shown in the two pictures took place. Can you think of some of them?

6 Why do you think the remains of dead birds were fixed to the wall of the barn?

a Engraving of a farming scene

1 Make a list of all the activities in Picture *a*. How many people can you see working at each activity? The table is started for you:

Activity	People working
Threshing corn with a flail in the barn	1 man
Shearing sheep	2 men

An agricultural country

Before the Industrial Revolution, Britain was an agricultural country. Although there were many small towns, most of the six and a half million people earned all or part of their living from the land. At times when grain prices were low, many small farmers sold out to larger landowners or to merchants who had made their fortunes in trade. These landowners wanted to farm more efficiently to get a higher rent from their land, and after 1660 farming methods gradually began to change.

New farming ideas

New ideas spread slowly. The term 'Agricultural Revolution' can be used to describe the changes which took place over a long period of time. In East Anglia, landowners began to try out the farming methods of the Dutch, who were the most advanced farmers in Europe. Growing turnips and clover as field crops to feed livestock was made popular by Sir Richard Weston and later by Lord 'Turnip' Townshend. The old three year rotation left one third of the land fallow (uncultivated) each year. The new Norfolk four course rotation used all the land. Wheat, turnips to clean the soil, barley, and clover to enrich the soil were grown. As a result more winter fodder was provided for livestock.

7　Identify the main features in Picture *b* by linking the letters (A — I) with the correct descriptions in the chart below:

Feature	Letter (A — I)
Two men on stack pitching sheaves	
Two men untying sheaves to hand to the feeder	
The feeder man	
Spout where the corn comes out	
Spout at which cobs are delivered	
Engine driver	
Apparatus for sorting types of corn	

b Eight-horse-power steam engine and threshing machine

8　Write down any questions you would like to ask about the two pictures. For example, why were so many people employed on farms in the past?

9　Try to find out answers to the questions you have asked in question 8.

10　Why was more food needed in the eighteenth and nineteenth centuries?

Farming machinery

Ploughs were improved and Jethro Tull, in his book *Horse Hoeing Husbandry*, described his seed planting horse drill and a horse-drawn hoe for weeding. The threshing machine was invented in 1785 but its use did not become widespread until the 1820s (Opening 3).

The population of Great Britain

The population had risen to almost eleven million by the time of the first census in 1801 and to over eighteen million by 1851. This increased the demand for food and helped to speed up farming changes. Robert Bakewell, a Leicestershire farmer, used scientific methods to breed sheep which could provide more meat and wool. The Colling brothers bred Durham shorthorns (cattle). Land-owners found farming more profitable and noble-men like Thomas Coke, Earl of Leicester, encouraged their tenant farmers to use the new methods. European visitors came to the farming and sheep-shearing festivals which Coke organized. King George III ('Farmer George') wrote about agriculture and set up a model farm at Windsor.

As a result of agricultural improvements Britain was able to feed a growing population. Without these changes the growth of towns and the Industrial Revolution could not have taken place.

2 Fencing the fields

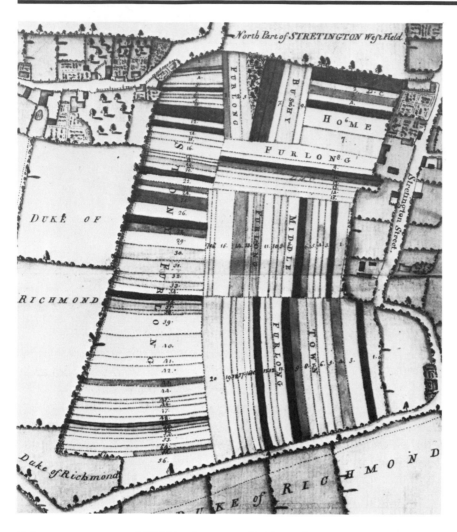

Private estate map (1781): the open fields at Stretington, Sussex

1   From the first map, who owned most of the land in Stretington?

2   How did his fields differ from other land in the village?
3   Can you suggest how Stony Furlong, Bushy Furlong, Town Furlong and Middle Furlong got their names?
4   Make a survey of the open fields by completing the chart below:

Field name	No. of strips
Home Furlong	15
Bushy Furlong	
Middle Furlong	
Town Furlong	
Stony Furlong	

5   Draw a simple plan of the village in order to complete the following exercise. You are living at the farm in the top right-hand corner. You farm a total of 15 strips in the 5 furlongs. Mark your own strips (you should not have more than three strips in any one furlong and no two strips should be together).

The old system
Under the old farming system the arable land in many villages was divided into strips scattered over three large open fields. Two of the fields were used for grain crops, while one field lay fallow in turn each year to recover its fertility. Around the village was the common land where the villagers could graze animals and collect firewood.

What was enclosure?
The strips of land were joined together and surrounded (or enclosed) by hedges and fences. Sometimes the common land was cleared for ploughing. The reason for the change was that with larger fields, people believed new farming methods could be introduced.

How was enclosure carried out?
At first, enclosure was carried out by the general agreement of farmers. They exchanged strips or pieces of land (closes) to make compact farms. During the eighteenth century enclosures were carried out more often by Acts of Parliament. More than 3000 Enclosure Acts were passed between 1760 and 1815. When an Act had been passed, the village to be enclosed would be visited by men called commissioners. The land which

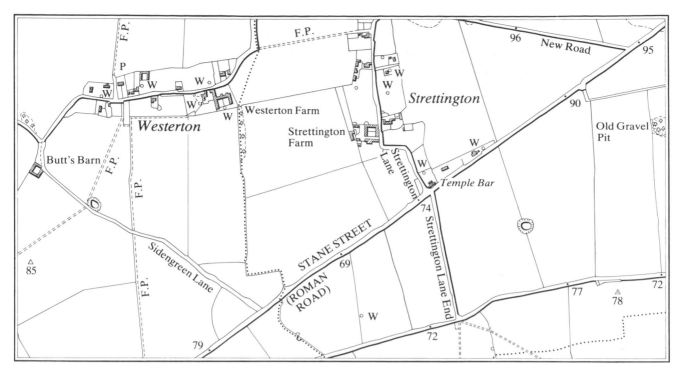

Strettington in the mid nineteenth century

6 Listed below are some of the disadvantages of open field farming. Rearrange the list, starting with the most serious disadvantage:

a Boots soon wear out with the amount of walking

b It is difficult to see all the strips in one day

c Some farmers have better land than others

d Much land is wasted by the footpaths and balks between each strip

e It looks untidy

f The farmers sometimes forget which strips are theirs

g Weeds can easily spread from one strip to another

7 What changes took place in Stretington between the times of the two maps?

8 Make a list of as many of the street names in the place where you live or go to school as you can. Then classify them under the headings below:

Local place names	
Examples	connected with:
Wood Lane	Land use
Red Hill	Natural features
West Field Lane	Former fields
Railway Terrace	Transport
Chapel Lane	Buildings
Pottery Lane	Industry

each farmer held in scattered strips was added together and some extra was usually given for his loss of common land to form a compact farm. The commissioners also fixed the village boundaries and decided where new roads would be needed.

Was enclosure fair?

Landowners hoped that the increased value of enclosed land would enable them to put up the rents of their tenant farmers. For example, Thomas Coke raised the annual rental of his estate from £2200 to over £20,000. When food prices were high, the tenant farmers could pay the high rents from the sale of their farm produce.

When food prices fell after the wars, tenants found it difficult to pay high rents and many were forced to leave their farms.

What were the results of enclosure?

Some of the poorer farmers were left with very small plots of land, which they often sold to the more wealthy landowners. The labourers who did not own land lost their rights on the common land. But compact farms replaced the open field strip system, improved farming methods spread through the country and more food could be produced for the growing population.

3 The agricultural labourers

PETITIONS.

HANG'D

PUNISHMENT IN ENGLAND FOR A BLOODLESS RIOT.

Decline and fall of an agricultural labourer

1 The five pictures above are not in order. *Either* write out the captions in the correct sequence *or* redraw them, to tell the story.
2 *Either* say to which pictures the following 'bubble' captions could be added, *or* draw them in on your picture strip:
   – Here's good roast beef for your table, husband
   – No mercy for those who riot
   – But I cannot keep my family on such a sum
   – Sir, we beg you to listen to our plight
   – Come lads, let's smash the machine

3 How does the artist show that life was becoming much harder for the labourer?
4 Was the artist on the side of: (*a*) the parish from whom relief was obtained (*b*) the Government whom the labourer petitioned, or (*c*) the labourer? Give reasons for your answer.
5 Do you think the labourer should have been hanged for smashing machinery and burning hay ricks? Give your reasons.

Movement of people from the land

In the eighteenth century the wages of farm labourers were very low. Attracted by higher wages, many people left the countryside for the towns, ports and growing industrial communities on the coalfields. Often the farm labourers and their families who remained on the land were under-employed and life became harder.

Changes in the standard of living

During the years of war against France (1793-1815) prices rose more rapidly than wages. Many labourers were forced to ask the parish authorities for assistance. In 1795 the local magistrates at Speenhamland in Berkshire decided that the wages of farm labourers could be added to out of the poor rates. The amount given depended on the size of the labourer's family and on the price of bread. The Speenhamland 'system' soon spread to other counties. As a result, actual wages remained low.

The Swing Riots

Grain had always been threshed by hand with a flail to separate the wheat from the chaff. It was hard work but it provided work during the winter. By using threshing machines, from the 1820s, the farmers did not need so many labourers. With

THE LIFE OF A LABOURER

CONTENT HAVING FOOD & RAIMENT

John Coulter Pauper two shillings weekly

BEGGARD BY MISGOVERNMENT AND RECEIVING ALMS OF THE PARISH

GRIPEALL'S THRASHING MACHINES

IN IGNORANCE TRIES TO RIGHT HIMSELF AND GETS

6 Using all the captions, write a short play.
   Characters:
   The labourer and his wife
   The parish overseer giving relief
   The Member of Parliament
   A manufacturer of farm machines
   Other labourers
   The judge at the labourer's trial
   The prosecution and the defence
   Scenes:
   A labourer's cottage
   Meeting of the parish authorities
   Visit of labourers to the house of a local MP
   Outside a threshing-machine maker's
   The courtroom at the trial of the labourers

7 What happened to the standard of living of
   many agricultural labourers in the late
   eighteenth and early nineteenth centuries?

less work to be found, the labourers rose in revolt, in what are called the Swing Riots. They demanded higher wages and the destruction of the threshing machines. Some machines were smashed and hay ricks were burned in several villages. The government and local magistrates dealt harshly with the rioters: nine were hanged and 450 transported to Australia.

The Tolpuddle Martyrs

In 1834 six farm labourers from Tolpuddle in Dorset were convicted of taking secret oaths when joining a local trade union. Again, the magistrates acted harshly and sentenced the 'martyrs' to be transported. It was hoped that the punishment would stop working men from joining trade unions. As there seemed little chance of improving their living conditions, many farm labourers moved to the towns or emigrated. The worst poverty was in the south of England.

4 The domestic system

1 Write out the captions under the two apprentices.
2 Make two columns, one for the idle and the other for the industrious apprentice, like those opposite. Place the numbered items underneath in the correct column, by looking carefully at the picture.

The idle apprentice	The industrious apprentice
Beer tankard (1)	Busy working at loom with shuttle (8)

cat playing with shuttle (9);
pipe (3);
the ballad of Dick Whittington, lord mayor of London (6);
apprentice asleep (7);
the ballad of Moll Flanders, a criminal (4);
the apprentice's guide, in good condition (5);
the apprentice's guide, torn up (2)

3 Hogarth has suggested the future for each apprentice: a hangman's rope; and the mace of the lord mayor. Can you suggest what he is trying to show?

Two apprentices at their weaving looms, by Hogarth

What was the domestic system?

Apart from farming, the largest industry in Britain was the manufacture of textiles — woollen cloth, worsteds, linen, silk and cotton. In the early eighteenth century there were no factories, and goods were made by hand. The simplest processes were carried out in people's own homes. After working on the land, many families then made cloth in their cottages, using simple machines. In the woollen industry, the younger children carded or straightened the wool fibres. The fibres were then spun into a continuous thread or yarn on hand spinning wheels by the women in the family. The men then wove the spun yarn into cloth, on a simple handloom. They worked long hours, earned low wages, and at some times of the year there was not enough work. This system of work at home is usually called 'domestic industry', or 'cottage industry'.

The finishing processes

This stage was usually controlled by cloth merchants. The natural grease was washed from the woollen cloth after it had been woven. It could then be bleached or dyed if coloured cloth was required. The cloth also had to be finished by raising the nap (fibres) to improve its quality and appearance.

Croppers at a workshop near Huddersfield

4 Identify all the activities in the cropping room by matching each number in the picture with the correct description below. One example is given:

Description	Number
Examining the cloth for faults	4
Dampening the cloth to crop it wet	
Two containers (empty) in which rough cloth was brought from the market or fulling mill	
Cropping with shears	
Raising the cloth before cropping	
Mossing the cloth with a handle set with teazles, after cropping	

5 The jobs in the table are not in order. Write them out in the correct order (start at the left-hand side of the picture and move to the right).

6 What kind of floor did the workshop have? What is the man at the front of the picture sitting on?

7 Did the workers wear any special clothing or footwear?

8 How were all members of the family employed under the domestic system?

Changes in the woollen and worsted industries

By the end of the eighteenth century, the West Riding of Yorkshire had become the most important woollen and worsted manufacturing region. The West Riding had coal, water power, soft water, cheap labour and river transport. The woollen industry was slow to use new machines. For example, the croppers (workers in the finishing process) were opposed to machines which might mean that fewer people were employed. The domestic system survived for many years in the woollen industry. More rapid progress was made in worsteds, which was largely a factory industry by the mid nineteenth century. In the case of the woollen industry, a complete factory system was not finally established until the 1870s.

Other textiles

There were other textile fabrics also made under the domestic system before the Industrial Revolution. Silk was made in London and in a number of Midland towns. In 1719 Thomas Lombe set up a water-driven silk spinning factory in Derby, but the real breakthrough in factory production did not come for another fifty years.

5 The textile revolution

Children in the winding room of a cotton mill (1820)

The cotton industry

The cotton industry started in Lancashire in the seventeenth century. Pure cotton goods could not be made on a large scale so fine quality muslins were imported from India. The government feared foreign competition and stopped the import of Indian cottons. However, the new fabrics had become fashionable and this gave the English cotton industry a chance to expand.

Textile inventions

The widespread use of John Kay's flying shuttle speeded up handloom weaving from the 1760s. More spun yarn was needed to supply the weavers.

However spinners could only produce one thread at a time using the spinning wheel. The world's first successful spinning machine was patented in 1770 by James Hargreaves of Blackburn. His 'spinning jenny' fitted easily into the domestic system. Its use increased the output of the individual spinner by about sixteen times.

Spinning factories

Richard Arkwright patented the 'water frame' in 1769, which used water power to produce spun yarn. In 1771 Arkwright set up a water-driven factory at Cromford on the River Derwent, which employed 300 people. Factories were built in

1 What scenes do the two pictures on this Opening show? Are there any similarities?
2 In which mill would you have preferred to work, and why?
3 In which mill do you think accidents were more likely to occur and why?
4 Make a list of all the differences you can see between the two pictures.
5 Can you give any reasons for the differences between the two mills?
6 Write a report (as a factory inspector) on the mill of 1840 and its work-people. (Include details of the child 'scavenger', who collected flying fragments of cotton from the machines and from the floor that might have caused the work to slow down or stop.) List the improvements which you think should be carried out.
7 List five questions which you would like to ask about the pictures.
8 Try to find out the answers to the questions you have asked from books in your library.
9 Which inventions helped to bring about the factory system?

'Working in a Cotton Spinning Mill' — an engraving from the novel by Frances Trollope, The Life and Adventures of Michael Armstrong (1840)

other parts of the east Midlands and in Lancashire, where there were fast-flowing streams for power. Some millowners employed pauper children, brought in from workhouses as far away as London. Samuel Crompton invented the spinning mule in 1779. It produced high quality yarn, but needed skilled labour to work it. So factories were also built in the towns, where skilled workers could be found.

Factory conditions

Although wages were usually higher in factories than under the domestic system, the workers disliked the strict discipline. People had to work long hours and women and children were often ill-treated by factory overseers. The factories were poorly ventilated, disease was common in the workers and there were many accidents.

Progress in power loom weaving

Progress in weaving machinery was much slower than in spinning. By the 1780s so much yarn was being produced by the spinning machinery that the weavers could not keep pace. In 1785 a clergyman called Edmund Cartwright invented a power-driven loom but it was not until the 1820s that technical improvements allowed the power loom to replace the handloom.

6 Slave labour

The daily toil of English factory 'slaves'

1 Write out what each of the characters in the cartoon above is saying.
2 How are the children being treated?
3 Do you think the cartoonist, Cruikshank, supported or opposed the employment of children in factories?
4 Why and how were working conditions for children improved in the factories?

The conditions of factory work

Even good employers made children work from 6 a.m. to 7 p.m. with only an hour for meals. In the worst mills there might be a working day of 15 hours. Children were employed as machine-minders, and cleaned and oiled the parts of machinery the adults could not reach. Sometimes overseers were paid according to the amount of work done by the women and children, so they goaded them to work faster.

Robert Owen

There were some reformers who protested. Robert Owen showed at his New Lanark Mills that manufacturers could treat their workers well and still make a profit. He improved his workers' houses, built schools and even provided a communal wash-house. Owen and another reforming cotton manufacturer, Sir Robert Peel the elder, promoted two Acts of Parliament to protect children. These Acts were not successfully put into practice and many factory owners continued to make mill-hands work long hours.

'Yorkshire slavery'

After 1830 the movement to improve factory conditions grew. Lord Shaftesbury devoted much of his wealth to improving the living and working

Attitudes to slavery as seen in McLean's Monthly Sheet of Caricatures: The Looking Glass *(1830)*

5   The picture on this page shows five different attitudes to slavery. How did each of the characters think they were right in their attitudes?
The slave owner argued that he could treat the slaves as he liked because. . . .
The Governor did not want to punish the slave owner because. . . .
The English Parliament and some MPs did not want to criticize the Governor because. . . .

6   What similarities are there between this cartoon and the cartoon on factory children (Opening 5)?

7   When was slavery abolished in the colonies?

conditions of children. Under an Act of 1833 no children under 9 years of age were to be employed in cotton factories and working hours were cut for older children. Inspectors were appointed to see that the factory owners did not break the new rules. By 1850 a ten-hour working day had been established for all workers in textile factories.

Slavery in the colonies

During the eighteenth century British merchants were involved in the slave trade across the Atlantic. They carried thousands of black slaves from Africa to America and the West Indies. Conditions on the ships were very bad and many slaves died on the way. Those who survived had to work on the sugar and cotton plantations, to provide the raw materials for British industry.

There was protest in Parliament, and in 1807 the trading of slaves was abolished. William Wilberforce continued to argue for the abolition of slavery itself. Shortly before his death in 1833 an Act was passed to free all slaves in Britain's colonies. The slave owners were given £20 million between them to compensate them for the loss of their 'property'. Finally in 1865 slavery was abolished throughout the southern states of the USA.

7 Changes at the coal face

A watercolour showing the pit-head of a coal mine (1820)

1 List all the ways in which coal is being moved above ground. Which method do you consider best? Say why.
2 Was winding carried out at the mine shown above: (*a*) by horse (*b*) by water or (*c*) by a Newcomen steam engine? (See Opening 9.)
3 What evidence can you find that some care was taken of the horses?

The demand for coal

By 1700 almost all the British coalfields were being worked. Most coal was used in homes but some industries — brewing, soap-making, sugar-refining, brick-making, pottery, glass-making and salt-making — were using coal or coke as fuel. During the eighteenth century more coal was needed to supply the growing towns and industries. The iron industry for example began to use coke rather than charcoal for smelting.

How did coal mining change?

As more coal was mined, the collieries became larger and deeper. This created problems of flooding and ventilation. The draining of flood water from deeper mines was made easier by the pumping engines invented by Thomas Savery and Thomas Newcomen. Ventilation underground was sometimes improved by using more than one shaft, and lighting a fire at the bottom to create a draft which helped the air to circulate. In some of the larger collieries ponies were used underground to pull the wagons along cast iron rails. Transport improvements on the surface meant that coal could be carried along rivers, canals, wagonways and railways, even from remote areas.

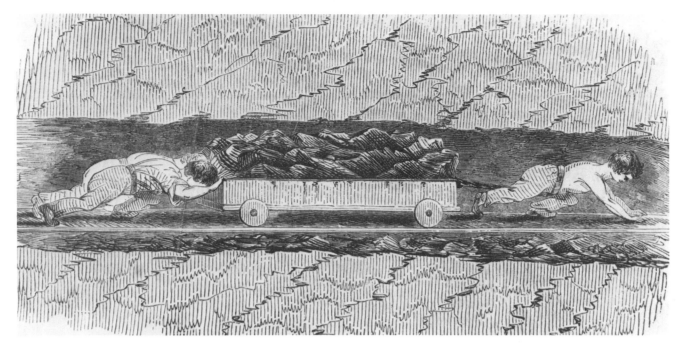

Children hauling coal underground

A Staffordshire colliery in the mid nineteenth century

4 What are the main differences between the two scenes underground? Explain the differences.

5 Which job would you have been given as a child?

6 How was coal moved underground at each stage of mining?

7 What tools and what means of lighting was used? Why might this be dangerous?

8 Write a report as if you were an inspector of mines on how children were employed underground. List the improvements which you think should be carried out.

9 How and why did coal mining change in the eighteenth and nineteenth centuries?

The miners

Some mining villages had little contact with the outside world. The lives of the miners were often controlled by powerful colliery owners who owned the miners' cottages. Women were employed and sometimes children from 6 years of age worked as trappers. They sat in the darkness and damp, opening and closing the trap doors which connected the underground galleries. Sometimes women and children carried the coal along narrow 'galleries' (passages) or tended the ponies.

Working conditions

Mining was a dangerous occupation and many lives were lost underground. Gas explosions could be sparked off by the candles used for lighting. Pits had few safety measures and it was not until 1815 that Sir Humphry Davy invented a safety lamp. This lessened the danger of gas explosions by surrounding the naked flame with a wire gauze. In 1842 an illustrated report on the mines showed women and children working in poor conditions underground, and shocked the public. Partly through the efforts of Lord Shaftesbury, a Mines Act was passed which banned the employment of women and young children underground.

8 The new iron age

The smelting works at Coalbrookdale (1758)

1   Identify the main features of Coalbrookdale by linking the numbers in the picture with the correct descriptions in the chart:

Feature	Number
The River Severn The ironworks Making charcoal Woodland A two-horse wagon bringing in coal or iron	

2   List all the ways in which goods and people are being carried.

3   At which time of the year was the engraving made?
4   Why was this a good time for carrying goods such as the boiler shown in the foreground?
5   What evidence is there that the boiler was very heavy?
6   What effects might the carriage of such goods have on the roads?
7   Why were the wheels of the wagon very broad?

A fuel crisis

Iron-making involved a number of processes. Charcoal fuel was mixed with iron ore and limestone for smelting in a blast furnace to remove the impurities. Because the smelted iron looked like a litter of piglets it was called pig iron. To make cast iron, the pig iron was melted again with charcoal and cast into the shapes needed. From the mid seventeenth century the timber used for making charcoal was running out and an alternative fuel was needed.

The breakthrough

A new discovery was made by Abraham Darby in 1709. His ironworks at Coalbrookdale in Shropshire used local coal, iron, charcoal, water power and water transport. Darby used coke instead of charcoal to smelt pig iron and to make cast iron. Coke is made from coal, of which Britain had large reserves. Darby's methods did not become widespread until the 1760s but the process meant that large quantities of cheap cast iron could be made. However cast iron is brittle and to make purer wrought iron was still costly and required charcoal and water power.

'The Forge' — an engraving by James Sharples from his painting of 1847

8 Look very carefully at the picture of the forge for one minute. Then cover over the picture and try to answer the following questions:

a) How many people were working in the forge?

b) What evidence is there that it was very hot in the forge?

c) What special clothing did the workers wear?

9 The engraver of the forge was himself a former blacksmith and forge-worker. How might that affect the way he produced his picture?

10 What are the main industries in the town in which you live? Try to find out which products are made and when the industries were started.

Wrought iron was made by removing more impurities from pig iron. It was a lengthy process which required prolonged hammering. In 1784 Henry Cort used coke to burn out the impurities of molten iron in the furnace. As the iron was being heated it was stirred or *puddled* with long metal rods, and the purified metal was passed through rollers to make plates or bars. Cort's *puddling and rolling process* meant that wrought iron could be made using coal and steam power. So by the end of the eighteenth century the iron industry was becoming centred on the coalfields.

New uses for iron

Because of the growth in population and the changes in transport and industry the demand for iron increased. The industry grew rapidly during years of war when iron was needed for armaments and weapons. Led by ironmasters like John ('Iron-Mad') Wilkinson many new uses were found for iron, including iron boats, cables, and ironwork in the water and gas industries. Perhaps most famous was Ironbridge in Shropshire, the first iron bridge in the world. During the nineteenth century, technical progress continued.

9 The steam engine

REFERENCES

By Figures, to the several Members.

1 The Fire Mouth under the Boyler with a Lid or Door.
2 The Boyler 5 Feet, 6 Inches Diameter, 6 Feet 1 Inch high, the Cylindrical part 4 Feet 4 Inches, Content near 13 Hogsheads.
3 The Neck or Throat betwixt the Boyler and the Great Cylinder.
4 A Brass Cylinder 7 Feet 10 Inches high, 21 Inches Diameter, to Rarifie and Condense the Steam.
5 The Pipe which contains the Buoy, 4 Inches Diameter.
6 The Master Pipe that Supplies all the Offices, 4 Inches Diameter.
7 The Injecting Pipe fill'd by the Master Pipe 6, and stopp'd by a Valve.
8 The Sinking Pipe, 4 Inches Diameter, that carries off the hot Water or Steam.
9 A Replenishing Pipe to the Boyler as it wastes with a Cock.
10 A Large Pipe with a Valve to carry the Steam out of Door.
11 The Regulator moved by the 2 Y y and they by the Beam, 12.
12 The Sliding Beam mov'd by the little Arch of the great Beam.
13 Scoggen and his Mate who work Double to the Buy, Y is the Axis of him.
14 The great Y that moves the little y and Regulator, 15 and 11 by the Beam 12.
15 The little y, guided by a Rod of Iron from the Regulator.
16 The Injecting Hammer or F that moves upon it's Axis in the Barge 17.
17 Which Barge has a leaking Pipe, besides the Valve nam'd in No 7.
18 The Leaking Pipe 1 Inch Diameter, the Water falls into the Well.
19 A Snifting Bason with a Cock, to fill or cover the Air Valve with Water.
20 The Waste Pipe that carries off the Water from the Piston.
21 A Pipe which covers the Piston with a Cock.
22 The Great Sommers that Support the House and Engine.
23 A Lead Cystern, 2 Feet square, fill'd by the Master Pipe 6.
24 The Waste Pipe to that Cystern.
25 The Great Ballanc'd Beam that Works the whole Engine.
26 The Two Arches of the Great Ballanced Beam
27 Two Wooden Frames to stop the Force of the Great Ballanced Beam.
28 The Little Arch of the Great Ballanc'd Beam that moves the No 12.
29 Two Chains fix'd to the Little Arch, one draws down, the other up.
30 Stays to the great Arches of the Ballanc'd Beam.
31 Strong Barrs of Iron which go through the Arches and secure the Chains.
32 Large Pins of Iron going through the Arch to stop the Force of the Beam.
33 Very strong Chains fixed to Piston and the Plugg and both Arches.
34 Great Springs to stop the Force of the Great Ballanc'd Beam.
35 The Stair-Case from Bottom to the Top.
36 The Ash-hole under the Fire, even with the Surface of the Well.
37 The Door-Case to the Well that receives the Water from the Level.
38 A Stair-Case from the Fire to the Engine and to the Great Door-Case.
39 The Gable-End the Great Ballanc'd Beam goes through.
40 The Colepit-mouth 12 Feet or more above the Level.
41 The dividing of the Pump work into halves in the Pit.
42 The Mouth of the Pumps to the Level of the Well.
43 The Pump-work within the Pit.
44 A Large Cystern of Wood 25 Yards or half way down the Pit.
45 The Pump within the House that Furnishes all the Offices with Water.
46 The Floor over the Well.
47 The Great Door-Case 6 Feet square, to bring in the Boyler.
48 Stays to the Great Frame over the Pit.
49 The Wind to put them down gently or safely.
50 A Turn-Barrel over the Pit, which the Line goes round, not to flip.
51 The Gage-Pipe to know the Depth of the Water within the Boyler.
52 Two Cocks within the Pit to keep the Pump work moist.
53 A little Bench with a Bass to rest when they are weary.
54 A Man going to Replenish the Fire.
55 The Peck-Ax and Proaker.
56 The Centre or Axis of the Great Ballanc'd Beam, that Vibrates 12 times in a Minute & each stroke lifts up 10 Gall. of water 50 yards high.

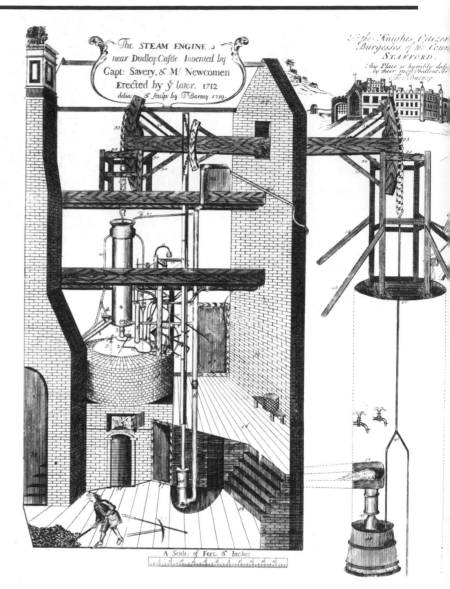

A Newcomen engine, drawn and labelled in 1712

Early engines

The most successful early engines were little more than pumps. Those invented by Thomas Savery and Thomas Newcomen in the early eighteenth century were used to drain tin and coal mines. The Newcomen engine worked by filling a cylinder with steam which was then condensed with cold water so that a partial vacuum was created and the atmospheric pressure drove the piston down. However, the steam was condensed inside the cylinder and needed constant re-heating, which used a lot of fuel. This engine was used in mining, in blast furnaces and for pumping town drinking water.

James Watt

James Watt came from Greenock, and was a scientific instrument maker to Glasgow University. In 1764 he improved a model of a Newcomen engine so that it used less fuel. This was done by condensing the steam inside a separate condenser so that the cylinder remained hot all the time. Watt needed money and a skilled work force to make the model on a large scale. However, his first partnership with John Roebuck of the Carron ironworks failed. Watt then became a partner of Matthew Boulton, who was one of the leading ironmasters in Europe and owner of the Soho metal works in Birmingham. In 1776 the first

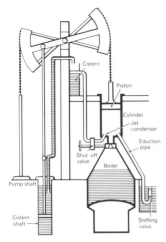

1 See if you can match any of the numbers on the 1712 diagram to the descriptions in the Reference list. Write out those you can identify, in modern language.

Detail from a print called 'Heaven and Earth' (1830)

2 Now look at the modern simplified diagram. The engine used expanding steam to push a piston up in the cylinder. What happened to the pump in the shaft when steam expanded in the cylinder (from right to left)? Did it move up or down?

3 What happened to the pump when steam in the cylinder was condensed with water from the cistern? Did it move up or down?

4 Using your answers to 2 and 3, describe how the Newcomen engine worked. (The beam vibrated up and down 12 times per minute and each stroke lifted 10 gallons of water from the coal mine from a depth of 150 yards.)

5 Using the scale on the 1712 diagram, calculate the length of the main beam at the top, which worked the whole engine.

6 Write out all the captions in the cartoon. *Example*, 'My good Voman, vot should you have Children for — don't you know there's no more hoperatives never wanted.'

7 Can you explain the connection the cartoonist makes between the use of steam power in industry; unemployment; people seeking poor relief; and increased sales of cheap gin?

8 Do you think the cartoonist is for or against the increased use of steam power?

9 Can you think of modern examples of technology which have caused unemployment?

---

satisfactory Boulton and Watt engine was patented. This improved form of pump was used in tin and coal mines.

The improved steam engine
When John ('Iron-Mad') Wilkinson patented a new method of boring cylinders, it became possible to make more reliable steam engines. In 1781 Watt and his foreman, William Murdock, made the rotary steam engine, which could turn a wheel and so drive machinery. Soon the rotary steam engine was being used in the pottery, brewing and flour milling industries and in the manufacture of iron. After 1785 steam gradually replaced water power in cotton spinning mills.

Why was steam power important?
Although water power continued to be used after the arrival of steam power, it had disadvantages. The level of water in streams varied at different times of the year and rivers were used for navigation as well. By using steam power, industry became dependent on coal. By 1800 there were about 500 Boulton and Watt steam engines in use which gave a great boost to the coal, iron and engineering industries. The use of steam power in spinning mills meant that factories were more often built on the coalfields.

10 The canal age

Barton Bridge, which carried the Bridgewater canal over the River Irwell (1794)

1 Identify the main features of the canals by linking the numbers in the picture above with the correct descriptions in the chart:

Feature	Number
The aqueduct	
The towpath	
The horses towing the canal boat	
A storeplace for goods	
A weir	
A water mill	

Why were canals built?

Britain's largest rivers had been used for navigation for centuries. However, the bends, silting and increasing mills meant that the rivers were no longer adequate for carrying bulky goods. Water transport was also needed in regions where there were no rivers. Canals had already been successfully used in Holland and France and many landowners, merchants and manufacturers in Britain were willing to invest money in this new form of transport. The first English canal, the Sankey Brook canal (1757), was built in Lancashire to open up the St Helens coalfield.

The Bridgewater canal

In 1759 an Act of Parliament allowed the Duke of Bridgewater to build a ten-mile canal from his coal mines at Worsley to Manchester. The canal was opened in 1761 and included a tunnel and the Barton aqueduct over the River Irwell. It was built by James Brindley, who also built the Trent and Mersey canal (1766-77). This 'Grand Trunk' canal became the most important part of the network of waterways designed to link the industrial Midlands with the ports of Liverpool, Hull, London and Bristol. It was financed by the Cheshire salt industry, the Severn Valley iron

The canal port of Stour Port (1776), at the terminus of two canals

2 What is the difference between an aqueduct and a bridge?

3 In what ways is the vessel on the river different from that on the canal?

4 How might the speed of the canal vessel be increased?

5 Which building materials were used in the construction of the aqueduct?

6 For what other purposes was the river used?

7 Using the picture of the canal port above, write an account for an eighteenth-century newspaper of the opening of Stourport, at the terminus of the Stafford and Worcester canals. Include a headline, details of the canals and boats, the people who might have attended, the weather, the musicians, and how you think the canal port will be useful.

8 Why were canals built in the eighteenth and nineteenth centuries?

9 Which is the nearest canal to your school? Is it still used, and for what purpose? Where does it begin and where does it end?

industry and the Staffordshire potteries, including the famous manufacturer, Josiah Wedgwood.

Why were canals important?

By 1850 Britain had nearly 4000 miles of waterways which carried coal, bulky raw materials, foodstuffs and manufactured goods. Industrial regions benefited, especially Birmingham which was the centre of the English canal network. Liverpool and other coastal and inland ports grew. Canal building increased the demand for bricks, stone, timber and iron and employed mobile workers – the 'navigators' or 'navvies'.

Why did canals decay?

Transport by barge was slow. The width of the locks and size of the vessels varied and it was often necessary to 'trans-ship' goods from one type of boat to another. This was expensive and caused delays. Canals were not popular with passengers and could not match stage coach speeds, although some canal companies used 'fly-boats' which changed towing horses frequently. Even before the coming of the railways some canals made little profit. Many more failed to meet railway competition.

11 Roads and road transport

A print by Thomas Bowles showing the street of Cornhill, London (1750)

1 Draw up a list of all the different ways in which goods and people were being carried in Cornhill, London. Are there any forms of transport shown which are still used today?
2 Make out a set of rules which might have made the streets of London more orderly in 1750. For example:
No herds of animals are to be driven during daylight hours.
3 Which noises might you have heard in Cornhill?

Road conditions in the seventeenth century

Most roads had no proper surface and were pitted with dangerous potholes. The local parish authorities were responsible for their repair and upkeep. The men of the parish were supposed to do six days' unpaid work on the local roads each year. The parishes on main roads found that it was impossible to carry out repairs and blamed 'strangers' and through-traffic for their ruinous state.

Turnpikes

One way of helping the parishes was to make all road-users pay. From 1663 onwards, Acts of Parliament gave groups of local landowners and merchants powers to improve the roads. These companies, known as turnpike trusts, put up toll gates and appointed toll-keepers to collect money from people using the road. Sometimes people objected to paying tolls and turnpike riots took place.

The main roads leading to and from London were among the first to be turnpiked. By the second half of the eighteenth century about forty turnpike Acts were passed each year and by the 1830s there were about 1100 turnpike trusts which controlled about 22,000 miles of road.

4 How do you know that
   the coach in the snowdrift
   carried mail?

5 Why has one lead horse
   been unharnessed and why
   has it left the road?

6 What is the rider carrying
   on his back?

7 The scene above is part of
   a story. Write about the
   events leading up to it and
   what happened afterwards.

8 In what ways was the
   coach in the snow different
   from the one travelling
   from Greenwich to
   Charing Cross?

9 How many of the following
   can you see on the Greenwich to Charing Cross
   coach: coachmen; outside
   passengers; inside
   passengers; dogs; musical
   instruments?

10 How had the two wayside
   beggars chosen a good
   position to wait for a
   coach?

11 How and why were roads
   improved in the eighteenth
   and nineteenth centuries?

Engraving showing a mail coach in a snowdrift (1825)

Passengers piled on the Greenwich to Charing Cross coach

Pioneers in road improvement

Despite his blindness, John 'Blind Jack' Metcalf improved many roads in Lancashire and Yorkshire by using solid foundations, drainage ditches, easy gradients and convex surfaces. Thomas Telford, a Scottish engineer, built roads, canals and docks. His work included the Menai Suspension Bridge between Anglesey and North Wales on his famous London—Holyhead road. Telford's roads were well built but expensive to construct. John McAdam, another Scottish engineer, constructed road surfaces more cheaply by using small broken stones which were bound together under the pressure of the traffic.

Travelling conditions

Even with the payment of tolls, it was usually cheaper and quicker to carry goods on the turnpike roads. Road improvements led to more reliable coach services between the growing towns, and freight costs fell. During the 1780s a network of mail coach services was begun, largely through the work of John Palmer of Bath. Passenger travel times between London and Glasgow were cut from two weeks in 1700 to two days in 1830.

From the 1830s onwards the coming of the railways provided a new and faster means of travel and the roads were once again neglected.

12 Railways

The opening of the Stockton and Darlington Railway

1 Identify the main features of the Stockton and Darlington Railway by linking the numbers in the picture with the correct descriptions in the table.
2 How was the first class coach different from the other coaches? What does it remind you of?
3 How could each wagon be stopped if necessary?

Feature	Number
Six wagons carrying coal	
The tender holding water	
The locomotive driver, George Stephenson	
The flag carrier announcing the locomotive	
The first class coach for important guests	
Other carriages for passengers	

The earliest railways

The earliest railways were built on the coalfields. Horses pulled the coal wagons on wooden rails to the rivers, especially the River Tyne. In 1767 Richard Reynolds built a cast iron track from Coalbrookdale to the River Severn. From the early nineteenth century wrought iron rails began to be used.

Experiments in steam locomotion

Steam became more worthwhile as the cost of horse power rose. Richard Trevithick built the first locomotive to run on rails for the carriage of coal and iron in South Wales. In 1808 he operated an engine, 'Catch Me Who Can', which ran on a circular track in London. Shortly afterwards William Hedley built the famous 'Puffing Billy'.

George Stephenson

When the colliery owners around Darlington planned a railway to the port of Stockton, they appointed George Stephenson as engineer. This railway was opened in 1825 and used both horses and steam. Stephenson drove the engine 'Locomotion 1' at the head of the first train. His work as engineer on the Liverpool and Manchester railway was even more important, when Stephenson's 'Rocket' was selected as the prize locomotive.

Lithograph cartoon showing 'The Effects of the Railroad on Brute Creation' (1831)

4　Write out all the captions in the cartoon.

5　What have all the horses' comments in common? What is the cartoonist trying to show?

6　Which people felt that they would lose their jobs as a result of the railways?

7　What were the main differences between travelling first, second and third class?

8　Which are the main railways in your region today? Mark them on a simple sketch map entitled 'Local railways'.

Different classes of rail travel as shown in the Illustrated London News *(1847)*

Railway development

Railway development was sometimes opposed by turnpike trusts, stage-coach companies and canal operators. Landowners sometimes objected to railways coming near their estates. A few towns, like Northampton, refused to be on a railway line. There were differences in the width of lines until an Act in 1846 made Stephenson's narrow gauge of 4 feet 8½ inches the standard, and not the 7 feet gauge which Isambard Kingdom Brunel had used in building the Great Western Railway.

Railways reduced transport costs, encouraged the carriage of bulky goods and foodstuffs, and provided cheaper passenger travel. New towns grew up as railway centres, for example Crewe and Swindon. The building of railways also employed many men — the navvies.

13 Inventions of the industrial age

Many of the inventors of the Industrial Revolution were also skilful mechanics. Others pioneered their first inventions using simple tools. Successful inventors and manufacturers probably had similar personal qualities. They worked hard and were determined to succeed and to overcome problems.

Using the information in this book, and other books in the school or local library, select the right answers to suggest how the following inventor—manufacturers succeeded. (Answers at the back of the book.)

1 In 1715, Thomas Lombe, a silk importer, heard that an improved silk spinning machine was in use in Italy. He soon became a leading manufacturer by:
   a) Asking the Italians to show him the machinery
   b) Purchasing machines from abroad
   c) Sending a relative to Italy on an 'industrial espionage' trip to spy out the secret of the machine

2 When a spinning wheel was knocked over in James Hargreaves's house in 1764 did he:
   a) Turn round the wheel as it lay on the floor
   b) Throw the machine out
   c) Scold the young people who had caused the accident

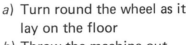

3 Hargreaves had to make his first 'spinning jenny' himself. Did he:
   a) Save money so that he could purchase tools
   b) Borrow tools from neighbouring spinners
   c) Use a simple pocket knife

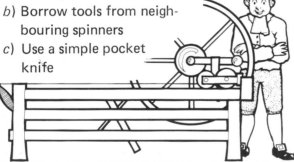

4 When Richard Arkwright, the Preston barber, met the mechanic Thomas Highs did he:
   a) Make him a new wig
   b) Ask him to construct a water frame and then copy the idea
   c) Ask him to teach engineering to the Arkwright family

5 Cotton manufacturers setting up textile mills in the 1770s had to consider many factors. Which of these was most important:
   a) Fast-flowing streams
   b) Sufficient numbers of local workers
   c) Availability of local coal

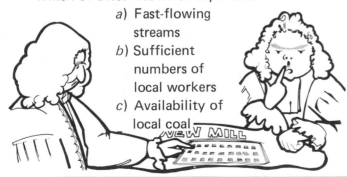

6 When Edmund Cartwright was told by several industrialists that it was impossible to make a steam power loom did he:
   a) Immediately start work on a weaving machine
   b) Look carefully at existing weaving looms
   c) Concentrate all his time on his work as a clergyman

7 When Robert Owen became manager of a textile mill at the age of 20 did he:

a) Arrive and leave on time

b) Always arrive first in the morning and leave last at night

c) Arrive and leave as he pleased to show his workers that the manager could decide his own working hours

8 If a machine-breaker or Luddite wished to make contact with other Luddites in a public house would he:

a) Ask the publican to announce if there were any Luddites in the inn

b) Put up a notice asking all the local Luddites to call round to his house

c) Raise his right hand over his right eye

9 If a pin-maker wanted to increase the output of pins greatly would he be best advised:

a) To employ more workers

b) To divide up the labour so that each worker became an expert in one process rather than the whole product

c) To purchase more advanced pin-making machinery

10 When Abraham Darby first moved to Coalbrookdale he was unsuccessful in using coal to smelt iron. So did he:

a) Try using charcoal instead of coal

b) Import all the iron he needed

c) Make the coal into coke first

11 James Brindley had many problems in canal engineering. Did he:

a) Work long hours (often through the night)

b) Read as much as possible

c) Go to bed thinking about the problems and waking up with the solutions

12 Did Josiah Wedgwood set up his famous pottery works on the banks of the Trent and Mersey canal because:

a) It made his pottery works look more pleasant

b) He was a keen fisherman

c) He wanted to transport raw materials and finished goods more easily

13 In 1780 gas has been suspected in a coal mine. As a coal owner would you:

a) Order the miners to use Davy's safety lamp

b) Send down a man with a canary

c) Abandon the mine to prevent possible loss of life

14 In 1836 the engineer Isambard Kingdom Brunel was 29 years old. He was working on ten important projects in docks, bridges and railways. If offered another project would he most likely:

a) Refuse the offer, saying that he was already engaged in too much work

b) Accept the new project

c) Suggest the name of another engineer

14 Medicine and science

A cartoon by James Gillray showing popular worries about modern medicine (1802)

1 Who published the cartoon?
2 Which kind of people did the cartoonist suggest might agree to be vaccinated against smallpox? Can you find evidence of any of their occupations? Were they rich or poor?

The rise in population
The rise in population was partly the result of a fall in the death rate. In the later eighteenth century there was a slight improvement in the standard of living. Changes in farming meant more food and a more varied diet, which gave added resistance to disease. The manufacture of cheap cotton clothes helped to improve hygiene.

Hospitals
Hospitals were built in many towns but conditions in them were often bad. However, some doctors were becoming more scientific and surgery was improved as a result of the work of John and William Hunter. The training of midwives was improved by William Smellie.

Smallpox
Inoculation against the 'killer disease' smallpox was made popular in England by Lady Mary Wortley Montagu, who had seen it used in Turkey. The patient was given a mild dose of the disease, which was inoculated into the arm with a needle. The patient became ill but inoculation prevented a more serious attack. Later, Dr Edward Jenner observed that milkmaids and farmers were often immune from smallpox after they had caught a mild disease called cowpox. When Jenner was sure

'Chemical Lectures' — An etching by Thomas Rowlandson (1810)

3   List all the ways in which the cartoon might frighten people against being vaccinated.

4   Why do you think the cartoonist has shown a picture on the wall of people worshipping at the feet of a cow?

5   What did Dr Edward Jenner claim was the main benefit of the cowpox?

6   How many members of your class have been vaccinated or inoculated? How is vaccination and inoculation performed today? Which disease do they protect against?

7   How was the lecture hall in the picture above lit?

8   Which kind of people attended the lectures? How can you tell that they regarded the lectures as a social occasion?

9   Which items of chemical apparatus do you recognize? Are any of these items still used today?

10   The lecturer shown in the picture invented a miner's safety lamp. Who is he?

---

of his findings he inoculated a small boy with cowpox, and later with smallpox germs, with no ill effects. Soon thousands of people were being vaccinated with Jenner's 'vaccine' (from the Latin word for cow).

Scurvy

Scurvy was a disease which struck many seamen on long voyages. It was caused by the lack of vitamin C contained in fresh fruit and in some vegetables. Captain James Cook, a famous explorer, prevented scurvy among his men by using lemons and limes and insisting on higher standards of cleanliness.

A scientific and technical age

Science was becoming divided into the separate branches of chemistry, physics and biology. Many industrialists and inventors practised scientific experiments. These included Josiah Wedgwood, an important pottery manufacturer, and James Watt, whose steam engine was the most important invention of the age. Joseph Priestley, a clergyman and writer, practised science as a hobby and was one of the first to discover oxygen. Sir Humphry Davy, who invented the miner's safety lamp, was a professor of chemistry.

15 Public health

Cartoon about the state of London water

1   The central figure in the Thames may represent Britannia. What do you notice about the trident and head-gear?

Why were the growing towns unhealthy?

The rapid growth of population, industrial change and inefficient local government meant that many towns were unhealthy places to live in. The most serious problem was the lack of pure water. Many water companies took their supplies from the rivers, which also served as sewers.

Cholera

Outbreaks of cholera occurred, with the horrific symptoms of severe vomiting and diarrhoea, but no one identified infected water supplies as the main carriers of the disease. In 1831-2 a cholera epidemic killed more than 32,000 people. The working classes who lived in the slums of London and the industrial towns were the hardest hit. Doctors and hospitals could not contain the epidemic and there were even rumours that cholera victims had been buried alive. The public were frightened of 'king cholera' and demanded public reform. In 1835 an Act led to the setting up of new town councils. Gradually these were able to remove some of the squalor, but it took many years to bring about improvements.

A drop of London water, as seen in Punch *magazine*

2 There are nine patches of dark water (opposite). What are these meant to show?

3 Write out all the 'balloon conversations' about London water.

4 What was the greatest fear of the London citizens?

5 Using the evidence in this Opening, prepare and design protest posters against impure drinking water.

6 Write a Health Inspector's report on the London street and the people who lived there. List the improvements which you consider necessary.

Poverty and slum living, as seen by the engraver Doré

7 How was public health improved in the nineteenth century?

8 If you can borrow a micro-scope, collect samples of the following to examine: (a) tap water (b) puddle water (c) pond water. Which sample resembles most closely the cartoon showing 'a drop of London water'?

Why did the government not take stronger action?
In the 1830s and 1840s reports on living conditions shocked the public. However, many people in power were influenced by the ideas of *laissez-faire* (leaving alone). Parliament was unwilling to interfere with the rights of individuals and of local authorities. For example, in 1845 a Bill to set up a Government department to supervise the supply of water and street cleaning was defeated in Parliament.

The Public Health Act 1848
In 1847 there was another serious outbreak of cholera. The following year, a Public Health Act was passed. This set up a Board of Health in London, which had the power to set up local Boards in places where the death rate was high. However, only a few local boards were set up. Edwin Chadwick, head of the central Board, became unpopular by trying to do too much too quickly. However he made the first efforts to clear some of the worst slums and to improve sanitary conditions so that cholera was stamped out. Yet much remained to be done.

16 The growth of towns

A cartoon of the first street lights in London, by Thomas Rowlandson (1809)

1 Write out the captions in the cartoon of Pall Mall.
2 Design the front page of a newspaper using one of the following headlines: 'New Light on the London Scene'; 'Gas Will Put Crime in the Shade'.

Towns
Before the Industrial Revolution towns were small. London, with a population of about 500,000, was the largest, but next in size Bristol and Norwich had only about 30,000 each. After the mid eighteenth century many people left the countryside for the towns, ports, and industrial communities on the coalfields of the Midlands, the North, and south Wales. They were attracted by higher wages and the opportunity of employment. Most of the movement was over short distances.

Immigration
Many Irish workers were employed in the building of canals, turnpike roads and railways. Others became handloom weavers and millhands. The Scots who moved into England were often skilled workers, and some became important manufacturers.

London
London grew rapidly between the 1780s and the 1820s. This was because trade increased, and because more people were gradually being employed in government. Much of London was rebuilt, but without an overall plan. New bridges

'The March of Bricks and Mortar' — a cartoon showing the spread of London's suburbs, by George Cruikshank (1829)

3 The cartoon above shows the growth of the city towards Hampstead. Which materials were used in the construction of many of the new houses?

4 Why were the houses built so close together?

5 What evidence can you find that the new houses were being built quickly?

6 How does the cartoonist show that the countryside was being destroyed by The March of Bricks and Mortar?

7 Which world-famous church can you see in the cartoon?

8 Find out about the development of your town and when the following were built or provided: the town's newspaper; railways; canals; main industries; town hall; gas and water works; bridge. Record them as 'Events' using the headings in the chart below:

Our town: Name			
Date	Population	Events	Illustration

were constructed across the River Thames, and London Bridge was rebuilt. In the centre of London, and some other towns, gas lighting was introduced, paving was improved and public buildings constructed.

Industrial towns

Industrial towns mushroomed as never before:

Town	Population	
	1801	1851
Manchester/Salford	100,000	367,000
Leeds	53,000	172,000
Bradford	13,000	104,000

Factory workers lived near the mills. The amounts they could afford to pay in rent were small. Many lived in rows of back-to-back houses, without proper ventilation; water was drawn from a communal pump in the street, and earth lavatories were often shared by a number of families. Paving, lighting and water supplies were often lacking, and many factory workers spent their leisure hours drinking, because cities offered no alternatives to the old festivities of village life.

17 Rich and poor

'Capital' and 'Labour' as seen in Punch *magazine*

1   Using the following information, write about the life of the rich merchant and his wife: servants; food and drink; clothes; pets; coach; leisure; home; large garden with fountains.
2   How did their lives differ from those of the 'underworld'?
3   Sacks of gold or money are shown in both parts of the cartoon. Can you explain the connection?

4   Make a chart to show the differences between 'capital' and 'labour'·

Rich	Poor
Servants employed	Servants of others

The rich and governing classes

The upper classes at the time were influenced by the ideas of Reverend Thomas Malthus, whose *Essay on Population* (1798) suggested that population grew faster than the food or goods which could be produced. The rich knew little of the lives of the poor and were more concerned about what to do with them than how to help them.

The Poor Law

Each parish had to take care of its own poor, and had the power to raise money through a special rate, called the poor rate. People who received help from the parish were known as paupers. In 1795 the magistrates in one Berkshire village decided that if a labourer's wages were not sufficient to live on he could ask the parish for an extra allowance. As a result, poor rates rose rapidly and wages remained low.

The New Poor Law

By the 1830s the Government had become concerned about the inefficiency of the poor law. Reformers such as Edwin Chadwick disliked a system in which men who were capable of work were able to draw assistance from the parish. It was not realized that most people who lived 'on the parish' were either elderly, poor children, or

'Tremendous Sacrifice!' — George Cruikshank's view of the sweating system in the 1840s

5 Write out the captions in the cartoon on 'the sweating system'.
6 Why was it possible to make clothing garments so cheaply?
7 If wages were so low, can you suggest why so many people were prepared to work under 'the sweating system'?
8 How did the Government try to discourage the poor from asking for assistance?

9 Try to find out about conditions of work in different occupations today. Build up charts like the one below with 'good news' and 'bad news' about different occupations:

The schoolteacher	
Good news	Bad news
Early finish to school day	Evenings spent in marking and preparation

those unable to find work. After the Poor Law Amendment Act of 1834 was passed, parishes were joined together to form Poor Law Unions. A workhouse was provided in each Union. Relief to the poor was only given inside the workhouse, and conditions were harsh to discourage people from asking for assistance. The New Poor Law was bitterly opposed. The amount of money paid out in poor relief fell, but the new system failed to solve the real problems of poverty and unemployment.

Co-operative schemes

Sometimes the working classes tried to improve their living conditions. One successful scheme began as a co-operative store in Rochdale, founded by 28 weavers in 1844. Each put £1 into the business and used the money to buy groceries at wholesale prices. These were sold at normal retail prices and the profits were shared out among the customers, as dividends. The 'co-op' gave ordinary people a chance to save. Soon other 'co-ops' appeared in other parts of the country as well.

18 Law and order

Two cartoons pointing out weaknesses in the night-watchman system

1 What is happening to the watchman or 'charley' in the first picture?
2 Do you think the watchmen could keep the peace in the growing towns?
3 Write out the captions in the cartoon 'Peeling a Charley'.
4 How does the uniform of the 'peelers' differ from that of modern policemen?
5 In what ways were the 'peelers' an improvement on the watchman system?
6 What improvements can you see in the street scene which might make crime less easy to commit than it had been?
7 What is the importance of Bow Street in the history of the police?

The constable and the watch

In the eighteenth century it was the duty of each parish to keep order among its own inhabitants. The Justices of the Peace or magistrates appointed the constable in each parish. He was an unpaid officer and had to serve for one year. In the larger towns watchmen were also employed. They served under the constable and did much of the patrolling. The watchmen were paid but it was often so little that the job was left to the elderly.

The Bow Street Runners

Faced with the problem of widespread crime, one London magistrate, Henry Fielding, built up a small force of detectives. These Bow Street Runners wore a uniform, and did much the same work as policemen on the beat. In 1792 Parliament passed an Act which set up seven police offices, using Bow Street as a model to follow.

A reward system

By offering rewards it was hoped that ordinary people would help the constables. An informer could receive from about £5 to about £40 for the conviction of a criminal. Citizens could also arrest a criminal. As towns grew in size it became more difficult to catch criminals. However, many people were afraid that if a new police system was

Bow Street and the peelers in the late 1830s

8 What is the importance of the following dates in the history of the police: 1792; 1829; 1833, 1835; 1856?

created it might be used by the government to curb people's freedom.

Robert Peel and the Metropolitan Police Force

When the Duke of Wellington became Prime Mininster in 1828 he wanted to reduce crime. The Home Secretary, Sir Robert Peel, persuaded Parliament to pass an Act in 1829 setting up a police force in London. Members of this Metropolitan Police Force were popularly called 'peelers' or 'bobbies' after the Home Secretary. This uniformed force was the start of the modern police.

The growth of the police force

In 1833 an Act was passed permitting any town which had a population of more than 5000 to appoint paid watchmen. In 1835 all boroughs were required to appoint a watch committee which, in its turn, appointed constables. A further Act in 1856 made the setting up of a police force compulsory in all parts of the country.

19 Crime and punishment

A labourer's wife begs the magistrate to release her husband with a verse: 'To soothe the rigour of the Laws, Let Beauty plead the Culprit's cause'

1 Link the numbers in the picture with each of the captions in the table, to show who says what:

Caption	Number
Caught in the act — the hare's but an hour dead.	1
Woof! Woof!	
What a bore these country yokels are, sister.	
What have you to say, man? Confess.	
This evidence must be written down.	
I do believe the man's starving, husband.	
And all done with a net.	
Send him for trial.	
But Sir, we cannot live on what he earns.	
It's enough to make one turn in one's grave.	

The criminal code

In the eighteenth century punishments included whipping and the pillory, but most offences were punishable by transportation or death. Parliament kept increasing the number of crimes punishable by death, until — in theory — a convicted person could be hanged for any one of 200 offences. Many of these were trivial, for example stealing something worth six shillings.

Transportation

Under the harsh Game Laws, the penalty for being found in possession of nets for rabbiting on open land was seven years' transportation to one of the penal colonies, like Botany Bay in Australia. But the strict penalties did not stop crime, because the police were not efficient enough to catch the criminals. Then the law courts were often reluctant to pass the death sentence for a trivial offence. So hanging was often changed to transportation. During the short time that he was Home Secretary (1828-30), Sir Robert Peel abolished the death penalty for more than 100 offences.

Prisons and prison conditions

In London the largest prison, Newgate, was specially built. But in many towns old castles or

2 Using the captions again, write the scene as a part of a play. Then write two other scenes, to show what happened before and after the events in the picture.

3 How does the artist show the poverty of the poacher and his family?

4 According to the law, what would have been the poacher's punishment?

5 Now look at the execution scene. How does the artist show that public executions were attended for entertainment?

6 What is the prisoner doing before his execution?

7 Write an account for a newspaper describing the scene and the events at the execution.

8 What were prison conditions like in the eighteenth century, and who tried to reform them?

'The Execution of the Idle Apprentice' — an engraving from a Hogarth drawing

toll booths were used instead, and these were often damp and without proper water supplies or sanitation. Disease was common among prisoners, especially the dreaded gaol fever. Gaolers were often unpaid but made their money from charging the prisoners fees or selling them alcohol. Until the nineteenth century, prisons were mainly used to detain debtors or to keep prisoners until their trial, or until the sentence was carried out. Not all those sentenced to transportation left the country; some were kept in floating prison ships or 'hulks' on the rivers Thames and Medway.

Prison reform

John Howard, sheriff of Bedfordshire, took a great interest in prison reform. He examined prisons in various parts of the country and argued the need for reform. Children were often herded in with hardened criminals, and in some prisons the inmates were chained to the floor, unable to move. The other great prison reformer of the period was Elizabeth Fry, who also collected up information. A devout Quaker, she visited the female prisoners in Newgate and tried to help them lead better lives. She succeeded in setting up a prison school, and also improved the conditions for transportees.

20 Schools and schooldays

The schoolroom at Harrow in the early nineteenth century

1 What evidence can you find that the pupils at Harrow school came from wealthy families?

2 What evidence can you find that the pupils who attended the London ragged school came from poor families?

Schools before the industrial age

Grammar schools and the great public schools, like Eton, Harrow and Winchester, taught mainly the classics — Latin and Greek. Private schools and academies grew in numbers and these taught more 'modern' subjects like mathematics, accounts and geography. Such schools were mainly for the middle and upper classes.

Schooling for the poor

Many poor children did not attend school. Others received education at dame schools, many of which were only child-minding establishments. Some charity schools were set up where poor children were encouraged to become honest, reliable workers and servants. Religion, reading, writing and arithmetic were the important subjects, although sometimes children were trained in occupations such as pin-making or shoemaking.

The growth and movement of population

The existing schools in manufacturing areas such as Lancashire, the West Riding of Yorkshire and the Midlands could not cope with the increase in population. But many children were employed in textile mills, coal mines, domestic service or farming, and parents on low incomes argued that they needed their children's earnings.

A ragged school in Whitechapel, London, in the mid nineteenth century

3 Make a comparison study in chart form between the two schools using the headings below. Include the following features: teachers; subjects being taught; forms of heating; pupils (numbers, age, sex).

Feature of school	
Harrow schoolroom	Whitechapel ragged school

4 Sketch all the teaching materials being used in the ragged school and label them.
5 What might a child at the ragged school have done during a school day?
6 In what ways is the Whitechapel school different from your school?
7 Are there any similarities between your school and the Whitechapel school?
8 How did schooling change as a result of the growth and movement of population?

Part-time schooling

From the 1780s Sunday schools existed and sometimes factory schools were started by reformers like Robert Owen. The 1833 Factory Act made part-time attendance at school a condition of employment.

Monitorial schools

Two voluntary societies, the Church of England National Society and the British and Foreign School Society, encouraged the development of new schools. These were monitorial schools, conducted in single, large schoolrooms where the master could keep an eye on the whole school at once. He instructed a number of older children — monitors — who in turn taught about ten children each.

The state and education

After 1830 the central government took a greater interest in schooling. In 1833 a grant of £20,000 was made to the two voluntary societies and this annual grant was increased to more than half a million pounds per annum by the mid nineteenth century.

21 A historical board game

Events

[1–10] Alfred scolded by cowherd's wife for burning the 'cakes'. Egbert (802-39) crowned as Britain's ruler or *Bretwalda*. Monk scourging a king at time of St Dunstan (909-988). Death of Ethelwulf (858) surrounded by churchmen. Alfred interested in the sea. Edmund the Martyr shows the Bible to the Danes (870). Saxon king buying off three Danish warriors. Guthrum the Dane makes peace with Alfred (878). Murder of Edmund during a feast (946). Danes destroying an English town.

[11–20] Torture of Queen Aelfgifu. Harold killed at Hastings (1066). Edgar (959-75) rowed on river Dee by other English kings. Edward the Confessor kneels before the churchmen. Blindfold woman tried by ordeal. Edward on horseback murdered watched by his stepmother (978). Edmund Ironside fights with Canute (1016). Harold entertained by William of Normandy (1064). Ethelred the Unready (978-1016) tries to buy off the Danes. Canute shows he cannot turn back the tide.

[21–30] William Wallace hanged in London (1306). William Rufus killed in New Forest (1100). Queen Matilda in the snow. Blondel plays harp outside Richard I's prison (1193). Execution of William I's opponents (1069). Murder of Thomas Becket (1170). Henry I told of his son's death (1120). Birth of Prince of Wales in Caernarvon Castle (1284). The Parliament of 1265. John at the feet of the churchmen.

[31-40] Execution of Ann Boleyn (1536). Princes smothered in the Tower (1483). Battle of Crecy (1346). Edward IV meets widow Elizabeth Woodville (1464). Peasants' Revolt and murder of Wat Tyler (1381). Henry VII crowned on Bosworth Field (1485). Death of John of Gaunt (1399). Henry V at Agincourt (1415). Wars of the Roses. John and Sebastian Cabot (1497).

[41-53] Napoleon I sent to St Helena (1815). Two Scots say farewell to Bonnie Prince Charlie (1746). Edward VI receives New Prayer Book (1549). Murder of Rizzio at side of Mary Queen of Scots (1566). George I sends his wife to prison. Burning of martyrs in Mary I's reign (1553-58). Arrest of Guy Fawkes (1605). Great Plague of London (1665). William III at Battle of the Boyne (1690). Trial of Charles I (1648). Quarrels of Whigs and Tories in Queen Anne's reign (1702-14). Cromwell dismisses the Long Parliament (1653). Charles II in disguise — Oak Apple Day.

You will need: or dice and a counter and sheet of paper for each player.

Player who throws highest dice number starts first.

Players move around the board according to dice scores.

Each time a player stops on a sq

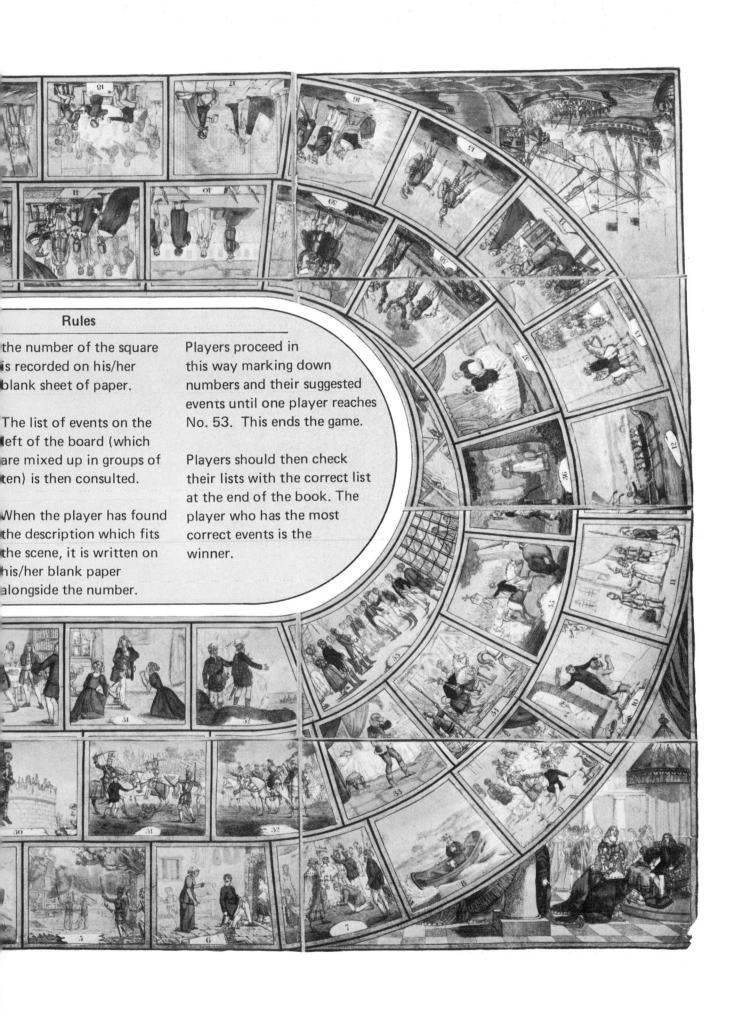

Rules

the number of the square is recorded on his/her blank sheet of paper.

The list of events on the left of the board (which are mixed up in groups of ten) is then consulted.

When the player has found the description which fits the scene, it is written on his/her blank paper alongside the number.

Players proceed in this way marking down numbers and their suggested events until one player reaches No. 53. This ends the game.

Players should then check their lists with the correct list at the end of the book. The player who has the most correct events is the winner.

22 The United Kingdom

The Crowns of England and Scotland

The two crowns had been united under the Stuart kings in the seventeenth century. However, it was not until the Union of Parliaments in 1707 that Scotland entered fully into the 'common market' of the English and made it the British Empire.

The Jacobites

The Jacobites supported the dethroned Stuart king James II (Latin *Jacobus* — James). They were strongest in the Highlands. James II's son, the 'Old Pretender', led a rebellion in Scotland and northern England in 1715, which was defeated by the armies of the English king George I (1714-

27). A more serious rebellion occurred in 1745-46 when the 'Young Pretender', Charles Edward Stuart, landed in Scotland. Scottish forces invaded England but were forced back and finally defeated at Culloden. For five months the Young Pretender wandered through the Highlands with a price of £30,000 on his head, before escaping to France.

The Industrial Revolution in Scotland

After the mid eighteenth century, Scotland entered a period of more rapid development. As trade expanded Glasgow and other towns grew and the Carron ironworks became one of the leading manufacturing centres in Britain. The

A contemporary cartoon of the Duke of Cumberland and the Young Pretender

1 The cartoon contrasts the Duke of Cumberland, who commanded the English army at Culloden, and the 'Young Pretender' (Bonnie Prince Charlie). Draw up a chart to show the differences between the two men:

The Royal British Hero (Duke of Cumberland)	The Frightened Italian Bravo (Bonnie Prince Charlie)
Write out his ideals according to the left panel	Write out his faults according to the right panel

2 Write out the verses at the foot of the cartoon. Underline the words which are used to show the weaknesses of the Young Pretender and his cause. Find out why Cumberland was nicknamed 'the Butcher'.
3 Design a cartoon in favour of Bonnie Prince Charlie.
4 Using a dictionary or reference book find out the meaning of the following terms: liberty; property; conscience; Magna Carta; Free Parliament.
5 Find out the meaning of the following terms: inquisition; arbitrary power; excommunication; popery.
6 What occurred in Scotland in the later eighteenth century?
7 Why did Ireland become united to England in the Act of Union?
8 Draw and colour the Union Jack flag. Label those parts of the flag which are made up of the original flags of England; Scotland; and Ireland.

most rapid growth occurred in the Lowlands where Edinburgh was largely rebuilt.

Ireland

Ireland was largely owned by English landlords, who obtained money from rents but who rarely visited that country. Most of the population were Roman Catholic but political power was in the hands of the Protestants who had their own Irish Parliament in Dublin between 1782 and 1800.

The Act of Union

Unrest in Ireland during the 1790s led to rebellion. The rebels hoped for support from France but a French invasion expedition was defeated. The English Prime Minister decided that Ireland could only be controlled if it was united with Great Britain. Large bribes were offered to members of the Dublin Parliament and the Act of Union (1800) created the United Kingdom. The Irish had been promised greater freedom for Roman Catholics but this did not come until 1829.

The Irish Famine

The Irish suffered a crippling disaster in 1845. In 1845 a potato blight hit their entire crop, and nearly three million died of hunger. Another one million emigrated to the USA or Britain.

23 The first British Empire

Clive to Mir Jafar, 17 June 1757.
3839 38 2920424 C'31 19342926 22181924
25193424 2238164 262335 192724 21
182322 1929 38 2423 192724 ? 2339
19164 241838322831 24193320 27193420
2339 2623353431201639 24181924 262335
1520 322324 353230233220 1526 2434201-
92718203426 152039233420 2926 1934-
438131916 1
Mir Jafar to Clive, 21 June 1757.
C'31 383224203224382332 3831 2423
18191320 183831 3832243420322718292-
03224 1924 292332273534419 241820-
342039233420 241820 31234322034 2623-
35 2919342718 2423 3919164 2332 1838-
29 241820 15202442034 1 22182032 2623-
35 27232920 32201934 38 311819164
24182032 1520 19151620 2423 14233832
262335 1 22182032 38 1929 193443-
8132030 32201934 241820 19342926 38
2238164 31203230 262335 253438131924
201626 19164 241820 383224201643828
20322720 1 162024 2920 18191320
2534201338233531 322324382720 2339
241820 24382920 262335 383224203230
2423 3938281824 1

Code

13 — v	24 — t	35 — u
14 — j	25 — p	36 — z
15 — b	26 — y	37 — q
16 — l	27 — c	38 — i
17 — x	28 — g	39 — f
18 — h	29 — m	1 — end of sentence
19 — a	30 — d	4 — repeat the letter
20 — e	31 — s	before. For
21 — and	32 — n	example 164
22 — w	33 — k	— ll
23 — o	34 — r	C — The Nabob

Secret code letters between Robert Clive and his ally, Mir Jafar, who had agreed to betray the Nabob, or Governor of Bengal, in the Battle of Plassey

1 Decode the letters between Clive and Mir Jafar. (*Check your versions with the correct ones at the back of the book.*)
2 Why did the power of the East India Company grow in India?
3 Identify the main features of the Siege of Quebec opposite, by linking the numbers in the picture with the correct descriptions below.

Feature	Number
The town and port of Quebec	
Five English vessels firing on the French positions	
English boats with infantrymen	
Infantrymen attacking a small French post	
The defenders of the French post	
The secret path which English infantrymen used to climb up the Heights of Abraham	
The English forces on the Plains of Abraham	

Trade and Empire

The growth of Britain's population and industry required more imported raw materials and more markets for the sale of British goods. Expanding overseas trade brought Britain into conflict with other European trading nations, especially France.

India

The East India Company was the most important of England's trading companies. It had 'factories' or warehouses in India at Calcutta, Madras, Surat and Bombay. Small trading posts had also been established by the French and Dutch. After 1740 there was growing conflict between the English and French East India Companies. Each side kept a small force of soldiers to protect their trading posts, and their trade in Indian cottons, muslins, spices and silks.

The Black Hole of Calcutta and Plassey

In 1756 the Indian ruler of Bengal was encouraged by the French to seize the British trading station in Calcutta. He succeeded but it was alleged that during the conflict 146 Europeans were packed into a tiny cell — the Black Hole of Calcutta — where 123 were suffocated. The East India Company's army, commanded by Robert Clive, re-took Calcutta, captured a French trading

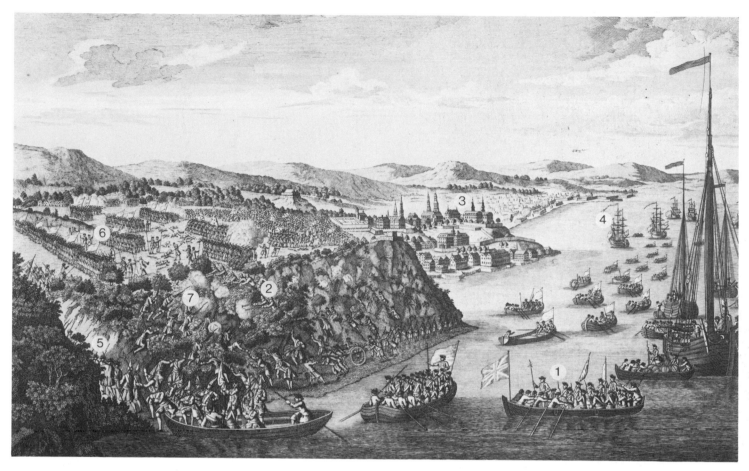

Contemporary engraving showing the capture of Quebec

4 Does the engraving show one, two or several different points in time?

5 How would a visual picture of a battle be shown today?

6 Draw a picture strip or diagram to show six different sequences in the Siege.

7 Why did the British want to capture Quebec?

---

station and then defeated the army of the Bengal prince at the battle of Plassey (1757). By 1760 French power in India had been destroyed.

Canada

By the mid eighteenth century the French controlled the St Lawrence and the Mississippi valleys. They began to build a line of forts between the two rivers, which would have prevented further expansion of the thirteen British colonies in America. To protect New England and the other colonies, Britain wanted to take Canada and control of the St Lawrence river from the French.

Quebec

On the St Lawrence was the capital of the French colony in Canada, Quebec. The French commander, Montcalm, was very skilful. The British general, James Wolfe, bombarded Quebec for four months but without success. Then the British discovered that it was possible to attack Quebec from another side. Wolfe and his army climbed a steep cliff route at night to get on to the Heights of Abraham above Quebec. The route was not well defended and the French were taken by surprise. Wolfe was killed at the moment of victory, shot by an English deserter, but his victory had won Canada for Britain.

A satirical letter, 'America to her mistaken Mother', published in an American political pamphlet in 1778

1 Decode the letter between 'America' and 'Britain' and write it out in full. The pictures form parts of words. The 'hieroglyphic letter' begins. . . (America) (toe) her (Miss)taken (Moth)er (Yew) s(eye)lly (old woman) t(hat) (yew) have sent a (lure) (toe) us is very (plane)

2 Now write out the translation in modern form, i.e.: America to her mistaken Mother: You silly old woman. That you have sent a lure to us is very plain. (*Check your version with the correct one at the back of the book.*)

The problem of the West

Following a Red Indian revolt, Britain proclaimed the American West closed to settlement. This annoyed those colonials who wanted to exploit the lands in the West. Then Britain also insisted that the Americans should pay taxes for protection by a large British force.

Taxation

A tax was placed on sugar and a stamp duty on all legal documents used in the colonies. The Americans argued that no taxation should be placed on them by the British Parliament in which they had no MPs to represent their interests ('No taxation without representation'). After riots and protests, the stamp duty was withdrawn. Further demonstrations against taxes occurred and five rioters were killed in the 'Boston Massacre' (1770). Britain removed duties on all commodities except tea. In 1773 a number of Bostonians, disguised as Red Indians, boarded British ships in Boston harbour and threw tea cargoes overboard ('The Boston Tea Party').

The Continental Congress

Delegates from the colonies met at Philadelphia to demand better treatment from the British government. The Congress became dominated by

The hieroglyphic letter reads approximately:

3000 miles [eye] have the fatigue of re[turn]ing [urn] after [horse]ing [hats] [coat] deserting t[legs] tired — [hats] [eye] of [pear] are [double-u][eye][eye] follow [urn] own[ed] [urn] [pear] gave [cup] me take home soldier [eye][ears] guard [hat] [urn] own tr[eagle][fly][louse] [ox] leave me [sole] my self as [eye] am at age [saw] know my own [eye]ntrests. [double-u]ithout [urn] [fish][harp] [ox] know t[heart] [eye][fish] [quill] [quill]ways. [egg]ard [pear] [ox] my Brothers as relat[eye]ons [barrel] [bow] as fr[eye]ends. [eye] am [urn][chair]ly [eye]njured

Daughter America.

3 The Red Indian woman drawn to show America has a flag with thirteen stripes and a shield with thirteen stars. What do you think these 'stars and stripes' were meant to show?

4 Draw the United States flag of today. What do the symbols represent?

5 The Red Indian woman is also holding a *fleur-de-lys*, the symbol of France. Can you explain the connection between France and the American colonies during the War of American Independence?

6 Try to make up a 'hieroglyphic letter' of your own to send to a friend. Invent your own symbols.

7 Why was there growing discontent in the American colonies in the years after 1760?

8 Draw a time-chart to show the main events in the American Revolution. Include the following dates: 1770; 1773; 1775; 1776; 1778; 1781; 1783. Use the headings below and complete a chart:

Date	Event	Importance
1770 1773		

a group of Colonial politicians who wanted complete independence from Britain. In 1775 British soldiers tried to seize arms in New England, with the result that the first military action of the American Revolution was fought at Lexington. Congress appointed George Washington as commander-in-chief of an American army. In 1776 Congress issued its Declaration of Independence from Britain.

War of American Independence (1775-83)
George Washington had difficulty in keeping his troops together and lost several battles. Britain found it difficult to plan a war which was taking place 3000 miles away. Britain was not opposed by all colonists and tried to keep some 'loyalists' on its side. In 1778 France and Spain came in to the war on the side of the Americans. In 1781 a British force was trapped between a French naval force and an American land force at Yorktown, and Britain was forced to surrender. At the Peace of Versailles (1783) Britain agreed to the independence of the American colonies.

25 Trafalgar and Waterloo

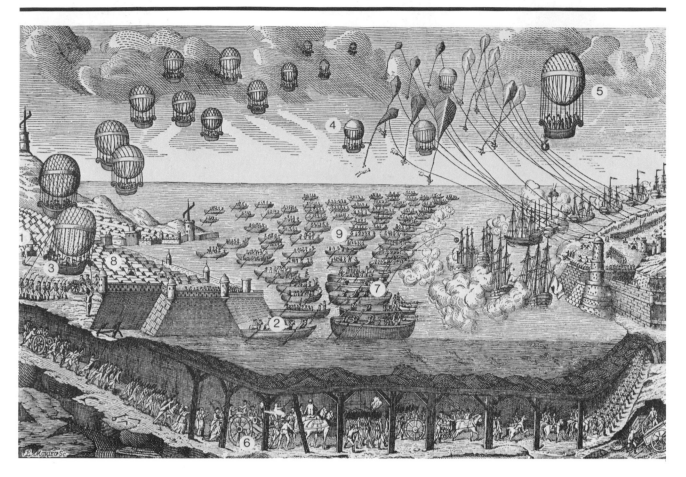

French projects for the invasion of England (1803)

1 The engraving shows an imaginary invasion of England. In which three ways does the artist show the French crossing the Channel?
2 Do you think the artist was an English or French supporter?
3 How has the artist exaggerated?

Britain and the French Revolution

The French Revolution began in 1789. In 1793 the French king and queen were accused of treason and guillotined, and many of the French nobility were massacred in Paris. In Britain, some people were horrified at what had happened, but others thought it right that the French people should demand justice and freedom for all. The French then invaded the Austrian Netherlands (Belgium), which threatened Britain's trade. Between 1793 and 1815 Britain and France were almost continually at war.

Trafalgar

Napoleon Bonaparte made himself Emperor of France. He decided to try to invade Britain, and gathered a large army at Boulogne and an armada of troop-carrying boats. In Britain, watch towers were built in case the French landed. Napoleon planned that the French and Spanish fleets should join together in the West Indies and then return to Europe and sweep the British navy from the Channel. But Horatio Nelson, the British admiral, met the French and Spanish fleets off Cape Trafalgar in October 1805, and won a great naval victory. Nelson himself was killed by a French

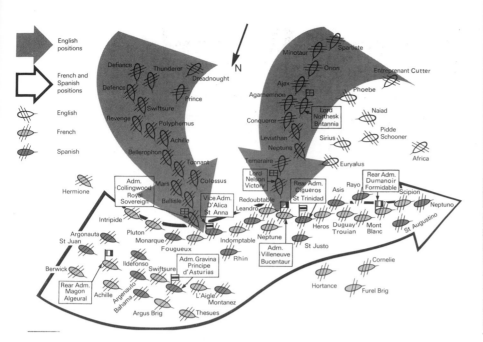

Plan showing the position of the battle fleets off Cape Trafalgar, 21 October 1805

Cartoon of a famous English general

4 Identify the main features of the imaginary invasion by linking the numbers in the picture with the correct descriptions below:

Feature	Number
The French army camped in tents near Boulogne	
The tent of the Emperor, Napoleon	
French troop-carrying vessels crossing the Channel	
Vessel transporting cavalry	
French transports firing on English defence ships	
A French balloon being launched	
A French balloon destroying an English balloon 'kite'	
French balloon which has broken through English air defences	
French artillery being moved under the Channel	

5 Now look at the plan of the battle fleets in 1805. Which sea battle ended the threat of a French invasion?
6 Which fleets took part in the Battle of Trafalgar? How many ships can you see on each side?
7 Which English general is shown in the cartoon?
8 In which famous battle did he defeat Napoleon?

sniper, but the danger of a French invasion was finally over.

Waterloo

To weaken Britain's trade, Napoleon then tried to close all continental ports to British ships. When Spain and Portugal refused to obey, the French invaded them, and British troops went down to defend them. After five years' fighting, the French were finally forced out of Spain. Napoleon was now faced by a coalition of Britain, Austria, Prussia and Russia, and was forced to abdicate. He went into exile on the island of Elba, but soon escaped and returned to France. Once again Napoleon gathered an army, and at Waterloo (1815) the French attacked the British army led by the Duke of Wellington. The French fought hard, the British defended well. Then, late in the day, the Prussians arrived and Napoleon was forced to surrender.

26 Peterloo: your verdict

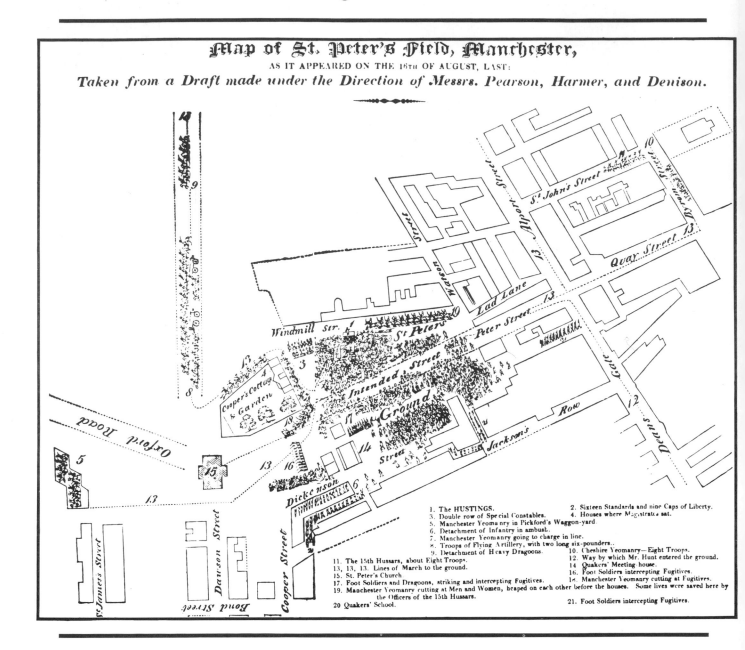

Map of St. Peter's Field, Manchester,
AS IT APPEARED ON THE 16TH OF AUGUST, LAST:
Taken from a Draft made under the Direction of Messrs. Pearson, Harmer, and Denison.

1. The HUSTINGS.
2. Sixteen Standards and nine Caps of Liberty.
3. Double row of Special Constables.
4. Houses where Magistrates sat.
5. Manchester Yeomanry in Pickford's Waggon-yard.
6. Detachment of Infantry in ambush.
7. Manchester Yeomanry going to charge in line.
8. Troops of Flying Artillery, with two long six-pounders..
9. Detachment of Heavy Dragoons.
10. Cheshire Yeomanry—Eight Troops.
11. The 15th Hussars, about Eight Troops.
12. Way by which Mr. Hunt entered the ground.
13, 13, 13. Lines of March to the ground.
14 Quakers' Meeting-house.
15. St. Peter's Church.
16. Foot Soldiers intercepting Fugitives.
17. Foot Soldiers and Dragoons, striking and intercepting Fugitives.
18. Manchester Yeomanry cutting at Fugitives.
19. Manchester Yeomanry cutting at Men and Women, heaped on each other before the houses. Some lives were saved here by the Officers of the 15th Hussars.
20 Quakers' School.
21. Foot Soldiers intercepting Fugitives.

Why were people discontented?

When the wars against France were over, the soldiers and sailors left the armed forces, but were faced with unemployment. The long wars had brought poverty to many European countries who were unable to buy British goods. The wars had been expensive and high taxation was imposed to pay for them. The poorer classes were hardest hit. As the prices of agricultural produce fell, many farmers were unable to pay their rents and went bankrupt. Unemployment rose among farm labourers and their wages were often reduced.

The Government

The Government feared that disturbances might lead to revolution, as had happened in France. Parliament was largely controlled by the land-owning and property-owning classes. Only a few of the middle classes and none of the working classes were allowed to vote, so the only way to voice their discontent was through disturbances.

Who wanted reform?

Political reformers such as William Cobbett and Henry Hunt demanded that Parliament should be reformed. Sometimes the unemployed and those whose jobs were threatened took direct action. In

The Marchers	
Time	Event
9.00 a.m. -12 noon	Arrival of 60,000 marchers (13) to hear demands for the reform of Parliament. Some marchers - men, women and children - carry Standards and Caps of Liberty (2). A few bring sticks and brick-bats
12.30 p.m.	Crowd sing national anthem around hustings (1)
About 1.p.m.	Main speaker, Henry Hunt, enters St Peter's Ground (12)
1.20 p.m.	Hunt reaches the hustings
1.30 p.m.	Hunt begins his speech (The reformers wanted to bring about the reform of Parliament; a fairer system of taxes; cheaper bread; freedom of the press; free speech)
About 1.45 p.m.	Crowd falls back and some panic as Manchester Yeomanry move in to arrest Hunt. Brick-bats thrown when Yeomanry try to seize Standards and Caps of Liberty (2)
1.45- 2.00 p.m.	Confusion. Many of crowd trampled as Ground cleared (19, 18, 17)
By 2.00 p.m.	The Ground is cleared leaving eleven of crowd killed and over 400 injured

Here is the timetable of events, on the day of a demonstration in Manchester in 1819, when the crowd of marchers was met by the local magistrates. There are two versions of the story.
1 What do you think really happened?
2 Who do you think was really to blame?
3 Could the massacre have been prevented?

The Magistrates	
Time	Event
11.00 a.m.	Magistrates meet at houses overlooking St Peter's Ground (4). Troops hidden near the Ground, Manchester Yeomanry in Pickford's Waggon-yard (5),15th Hussars and Cheshire Yeomanry at (11, 10). Infantry in ambush (6). Other troops and Heavy Dragoons (8, 9)
12 noon	Double row of Special Constables drawn up on the Ground (3). Magistrates read Riot Act (4)
About 1.15 p.m.	Several Manchester inhabitants sign statement that town is in danger. Magistrates sign warrants for arrest of Hunt and other leaders (4)
1.30 p.m.	Special Constables (3) inform the magistrates that they are too few in number (total 300) to arrest Hunt. Magistrates send messengers to ask for support from Manchester Yeomanry (5), and from 15th Hussars and Cheshire Yeomanry (11, 10). Infantry ordered to close in (6)
1.40 p.m.	Manchester Yeomanry arrive at the Ground (move from 5 to 7) and prepare to charge
About 1.45 p.m.	Arrest of Hunt and other speakers by Manchester Yeomanry and Special Constables. Panic in crowd when Yeomanry try to seize Standards and Caps of Liberty. Badly-trained Yeomanry unable to control crowd or their own horses. Some brick-bats thrown. Yeomanry uses sabres
1.50 p.m.	Magistrates (4) order well-trained regulars, the 15th Hussars, to assist Manchester Yeomanry and to disperse the crowd (19)

some parts of the country, machine-breakers (Luddites) destroyed new labour-saving machines. The Government made machine-breaking a capital crime, and several Luddites were hanged.

The disturbances
At Spa Fields in London a meeting of reformers turned into a riot when gunsmiths' shops were raided. The disturbance was put down by troops. In 1817 a march of Lancashire cotton workers to London was broken up and its leaders were arrested. In Manchester in 1819 a large meeting (which had been declared illegal) was held to demand the reform of Parliament. The local magistrates decided to arrest Henry 'Orator' Hunt and the other speakers but when the yeomanry tried to force their way through the crowd, eleven people were killed and many hundreds were injured. Following this 'Peterloo massacre' the Government passed stricter laws which made it more difficult to hold demonstrations.

When did conditions begin to improve?
Life in England slowly improved after 1820 and there was no further rioting for some years. Trade improved and unemployment fell. Many workers joined the growing trade unions, which were made legal in 1825.

27 The reform of Parliament

Freedom & Purity of Election !!! Showing the Necessity of Reform in the Close Boroughs.

A cartoon of the consequences
of voting against your landlord

1 Write out the 'bubble' captions from the two candidates.
2 The cartoonist shows one scene in a story. What do you think happened before and afterwards?

Why did Parliament need to be reformed?

Today the country is divided into areas called constituencies, each of which returns one MP. In the early nineteenth century, it was counties which sent two MPs to the House of Commons. They were elected by male 'freeholders', who owned land worth at least 40 shillings per annum. Other MPs were elected by 'boroughs', some of which were large towns where many property-owners were able to vote, and others were little more than villages, where the MPs were chosen by a handful of voters.

Many growing industrial towns such as Manchester, Birmingham, Leeds and Sheffield had large populations but no MPs, simply because they were not yet 'borough'. The situation in Scotland and Ireland was even worse than in England and Wales.

The struggle for reform

In 1830 a Whig government came into power, which was willing to promote a Bill for the reform of Partliament. However, the Bill failed to pass the House of Commons. A general election was held and the Whig party were again elected. A new Bill was passed by the House of Commons but thrown out of the House of Lords. There

Another cartoonist's view of the corruption at elections in the early nineteenth century

3 Link the additional captions below with the people numbered in the cartoon on the left:

Caption	Number
— I always paid the rent when I could. Surely a man may vote how he pleases? — I am too old to be turned out. — Voting against his lordship will not feed the two children. We have lost everything, husband. — But may we vote as we please at St Austle? — I'll not stay. I'll take my wife and three children to Canada.	

4 Now look at the second cartoon. How does the voting booth differ from a modern polling station?

5 Why do you think Gripes (198 votes) defeated Milksop (121 votes) at the election?

6 Do you think the cartoonists supported or opposed the voting system in the early nineteenth century?

7 When and why was the voting system reformed?

8 Conduct mock elections in class (a) under the electoral system in the early nineteenth century (b) under the present-day system.

---

were riots in many parts of the country for more and more people were determined to see Parliament reformed. The king, William IV, threatened to create enough new lords to make sure that the Bill passed, and finally the House of Lords gave in.

How was Parliament reformed?
The growing industrial towns were given more MPs, and the small boroughs fewer. The Act also extended the vote to the middle classes who owned property. It was a first stage of reform, which still left most of the working classes and nearly all women without the vote, and also the landowners still very strong in Parliament.

Chartism
In the 1830s and 1840s many working and middle class people turned to Chartism, a political movement which had a charter of Six Aims: voting rights for all adult males; secret voting; annual elections; the payment of MPs; constituencies of equal size; and the right of people to stand for Parliament without owning property.

The demands were presented to Parliament as monster petitions in 1838, 1842 and 1848, but they were rejected. Signatures were sometimes fictitious and the movement was ridiculed. But fortunately most of the Chartist demands were met by the end of the nineteenth century.

28 The workshop of the world

George Cruikshank's view of the British people, hard at work in 'The British Beehive'

1 How was the British Bee-hive defended?
2 In chart form, list the cells in the hive under group headings.

Class or group	Occupations
Servants and labourers	Cabman, etc.
Craftsmen	Glazier, etc.
Shopkeepers and trades-men	Butcher, etc.

3 Select two occupation 'cells' on any level which you think profited from the Industrial Revolution. Explain why.
4 Select one cell and write about the pleasant and disagreeable features of your life.
5 Do you think it would have been easy to move up from one layer in the bee-hive to another?

The first industrial nation

Britain was the first country to undergo an Industrial Revolution, and by the mid nineteenth century was the leading manufacturing nation in the world. Britain produced one-third of the world's shipping and manufactured goods, and had one-quarter of the world's trade. Largely as a result of the Industrial Revolution, Britain became a country where most of the people lived and worked in towns.

Benefits of industrial change

The changes in the eighteenth and nineteenth centuries enabled the country to support a growing population. After many years of distress, industrial change eventually brought a higher standard of living and improvements in the quality of life. The working classes grew in strength, partly through the activities of trade unions, friendly societies and the co-operative movement. The changes also affected the position of women in society. Working women gradually ceased to be employed as wage-earners in agriculture and began to be employed in industry and trade.

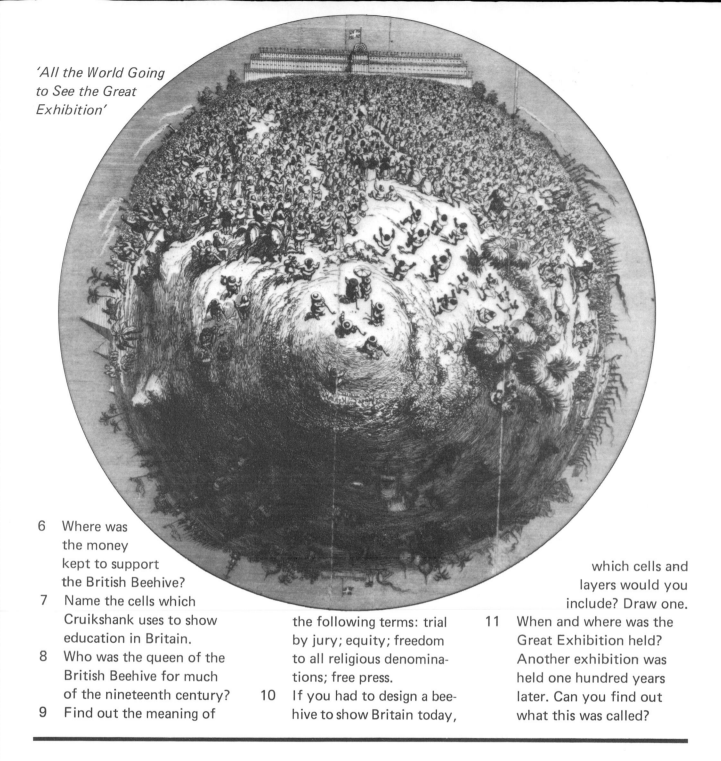

'All the World Going to See the Great Exhibition'

6 Where was the money kept to support the British Beehive?
7 Name the cells which Cruikshank uses to show education in Britain.
8 Who was the queen of the British Beehive for much of the nineteenth century?
9 Find out the meaning of the following terms: trial by jury; equity; freedom to all religious denominations; free press.
10 If you had to design a beehive to show Britain today, which cells and layers would you include? Draw one.
11 When and where was the Great Exhibition held? Another exhibition was held one hundred years later. Can you find out what this was called?

The Great Exhibition

Britain's new industries were put on show to the world in the Great Exhibition of 1851. The idea of the Exhibition was strongly supported by Queen Victoria's consort, Prince Albert. In Hyde Park in London, a great Crystal Palace was built. It was more than 600 yards long and housed more than 7000 exhibitors from abroad and as many from Britain. More than 6 million visitors came to the Exhibition from all parts of the world.

The cost of industrial change

To begin with, the changes in industry and the growth of towns caused distress to many of the population. The nineteenth century was an age of big cities with appalling living and working conditions in many of their districts. Yet it was also an age when improvements in some features of town life began.

Not all parts of Britain changed. In the Highlands of Scotland and in Ireland, a growing number of people were living on the land, which in the end failed to support them. The famine of the 1840s led to a heavy loss of life in such communities.

29 A day out

'Derby Day'. From an original painting by William Frith

1   Using the key below, write about a day at the Derby on Epsom Downs.

Key

1 Grandstand full of spectators
2 The course
3 Jockey in striped shirt and cap
4 Drinking tent
5 Betting table for a 'pea and thimble' game (in which gamblers attempt to guess which of three thimbles conceals a pea)
6 A schoolboy 'gentleman' who has lost his money on the game
7 A young farmer whose wife tries to stop him betting on the game
8 A tipster with a list of horses, shouting out the odds
9 A bare-foot flower girl
10 Gipsy woman begging from a lady with a parasol
11 A young boy stealing a bottle from under a coach
12 A hungry child acrobat looking at a picnic hamper being opened by a groom

---

Traditional entertainment: eighteenth century
Most entertainment took place on church and political holidays — Christmas, Plough Monday, Shrove Tuesday, May Day, Oak Apple Day and Guy Fawkes. On Sundays, fair days and feast days leisure activities were organized by the inhabitants of each community. Travelling performers provided additional entertainment. The inn was a centre for sport of all kinds, like cudgel-playing, skittles, bowling, quoits, wrestling, prize fighting and foot races. Football matches lasting several hours were sometimes played by whole villages. Cricket began to take on its modern form in the eighteenth century.

Animal sports and gambling
Fowling, fishing and shooting were popular among the gentry. Fox-hunting provided an opportunity for fashionable dressing-up and social activities, as well as for horse-riding. Most animal sports were centres of gambling. From the seventeenth century horse-racing was based on centres like Newmarket, Ascot and Epsom, where the Derby has been held for 200 years. It is said that the name of the race was decided by the toss of a coin, which was won by the Earl of Derby. Gambling was also widespread at the cruel animal sports, such as bull-baiting and cock-fighting. Large wagers were also placed on prize fighters.

2 Make a costume study by
drawing and labelling the
following:
— a gentleman in loose
flowing top coat with wide
lapels, a bright cravat and a
top hat with a veil or
'puggaree' to keep off sun,
dust and flies
— a lady in a crinoline dress
— a farmer in a smock
-- a farmer's wife with her
Paisley shawl
— a drummer showman with
moleskin coat and
bright waistcoat
— bare-footed gypsy boy in
ragged clothes

'The Londoners' Bank Holiday Outing' as shown in the Illustrated
London News *(1847)*

3 Can you name any of the famous landmarks
which the Londoners were passing on
their way to Greenwich?
4 How was the boat powered?
5 Which other vessels used the river?

6 How might a river trip be unpleasant?
7 What were the traditional forms of entertainment? Why did these decline in the nineteenth
century?

Fashion in towns

London and the spa towns such as Bath and
Cheltenham were centres for fashion and entertainment. In London there were elegant pleasure
gardens such as Ranelagh, Kensington and
Vauxhall. The River Thames was used for both
transport and for pleasure purposes. At times of
national celebration, for example a coronation or
a victory in war, there were bonfires and fire-
works. After 1780 ballooning became a craze, and
outdoor demonstrations of the newly discovered
electricity were organized. During the eighteenth
century, sea bathing became more popular, and
resorts such as Brighton, Weymouth and Scar-

borough grew in size. Many more resorts were
developed with the coming of the railways in
the years after 1830.

Nineteenth-century change

Many of the traditonal entertainments later went
into decline. The growing and respectable middle
class disliked the savage and cruel sports, and
attacked leisure pursuits held on Sundays. In
1824 the RSPCA was founded, and by 1850
cock-fighting and animal-baiting had been banned.
Gradually sports such as horse-racing, cricket and
boxing were becoming more orderly and subject
to 'rules of the game'.

30 The Great Exhibition

| 1786 | Threshing machine invented

THROW AGAIN. MOVE ON FOR EVEN SCORE, BACK FOR ODD | 1784 | England loses war of American Independence

GO BACK TO OUTBREAK OF WAR (1775) | 1782 | Watt invents rotary steam engine

ADD 3 TO NEXT SCORE | 1780 |

| 1787 | | | | | | |

Faraday discovers electro-magnetic rotation

MOVE ON TO 1823

| 1820 | Peterloo massacre

THROW A SIX TO MOVE ON | 1818 | 1817 | 181 |

| 1788 | | | | | |

| 1822 | | | | | | |

| 1823 | 1824 | Stockton and Darlington Railway opened

MOVE ON 1 PLACE | 1826 | 1827 |

Start of French Revolution

MISS ONE TURN

| 1790 | 1841 | Rowland Hill begins Penny post

MOVE ON 1 PLACE | 1839 | 1838 | 1837 | Mor deve |

THF

| 1791 | Mines Act

THROW AGAIN | | | | |

| 1792 | 1843 | 1844 | 1845 | Potato famine in Ireland

THROW ODD NUMBER TO MOVE ON | Cholera outbreak

GO BACK TO 1832 | Chartism fails

GO BACK 3 PLACES |

England at war with France

THROW A FOUR TO MOVE ON

| | British naval victory on 'Glorious first of June'

ADD 2 TO NEXT SCORE | 1795 | Jenner vaccinates against smallpox

THROW AGAIN | 1797 | 1798 | 1799 | 18 |

| 1751 | New style calendar introduced

THROW AGAIN | 1753 | 1754 | 1755 | Start of Seven Years War

GO BACK TO START | English win Battle of Plas

MOVE ON 3 PLACES |

START

| Crompton invents the spinning mule MOVE ON 1 PLACE | 1778 | 1777 | American Declaration of Independence MISS ONE TURN | 1775 | 1774 | Boston Tea Party GO BACK 4 PLACES |

1772

| Wellington defeats Napoleon at Waterloo THROW AGAIN | 1814 | Elizabeth Fry visits Newgate Prison MOVE ON 1 PLACE | 1812 | Luddites destroy machinery THROW DICE AND MOVE BACK SCORE |

1771

1810

| 1828 | Stephenson's 'Rocket' wins trials DOUBLE NEXT SCORE | Swing Riots Liverpool to Manchester railway opens GO BACK 3 PLACES AND THROW AGAIN | 1831 |

Boston Massacre

THROW A ONE TO MOVE ON

| First gas lights in London MOVE ON 1 PLACE |

1769

Cholera outbreak THROW DICE AND MOVE BACK SCORE

| 1835 | Tolpuddle Martyrs transported THROW A THREE TO MOVE ON | Slavery abolished DOUBLE SCORE ON NEXT THROW |

1808

Cook's first voyage of discovery THROW AGAIN

1767

1851

1850

ENTER THE GREAT EXHIBITION

1807

1806

1766

| Peace with France THROW AGAIN | England again at war with France THROW DICE AND MOVE BACK SCORE | 1803 | 1804 | Nelson wins naval battle of Trafalgar but is killed MOVE BACK 2 PLACES AND THROW AGAIN |

Americans oppose Stamp Act GO BACK 3 PLACES

| 58 | Wolfe captures Quebec but is killed MOVE BACK 4 PLACES THROW AGAIN | 1760 | Bridgewater canal opened MOVE ON 1 PLACE | 1762 | 1763 | Hargreaves invents spinning jenny DOUBLE SCORE ON NEXT THROW |

Acknowledgements

Every effort has been made to trace owners of copyright material, but in some cases this has not proved possible. The publisher would be glad to hear from any further copyright owners of material produced in the *Openings in History* series. The author and publisher are grateful to the following for their permission to reproduce illustrations, listed by Opening:

1 farm scene: Radio Times Hulton Picture Library; steam engine and threshing machine: Museum of English Rural Life, University of Reading

2 eighteenth-century map: Reproduced by courtesy of the Directors of the Goodwood Estate Company Ltd, with acknowledgements to the West Sussex Record Office and County Archivist; nineteenth-century map: Reproduced by permission of the British Library

3 Decline and fall of an agricultural labourer: Mansell Collection

4 apprentices: John Freeman; croppers: Tolson Memorial Museum, via Kirklees Metropolitan Council

5 winding/spinning cotton: Radio Times Hulton Picture Library

6 factory slaves: Mansell Collection; *The Looking Glass:* Reproduced by permission of the Trustees of the British Museum

7 pit-head/Staffordshire colliery: Radio Times Hulton Picture Library; children: Mansell Collection

8 Coalbrookdale: Radio Times Hulton Picture Library; 'The Forge': Blackburn Museum and art gallery

9 Newcomen engine: Science Museum, London; 'Heaven and Earth': Reproduced by permission of the Trustees of the British Museum

10 Barton Bridge: from J. Aiken, *A Description of the Country from Thirty to Forty Miles round Manchester*, David & Charles; Stour Port: Waterways Museum

11 Cornhill: by Thomas Bowles, Batsford; snowdrift: Reproduced by courtesy of the Post Office, Crown copyright; passengers on coach: Radio Times Hulton Picture Library

12 Stockton and Darlington Railway: Science Museum, London; 'The Effects of the Railroad': Radio Times Hulton Picture Library; types of accommodation: *Illustrated London News*

14 cartoon Chemical Lectures: Reproduced by permission of the Trustees of the British Museum

15 drop of water: Cribb Collection; poverty: Radio Times Hulton Picture Library

16 street lights/'Bricks and Mortar': Reproduced by permission of the Trustees of the British Museum

17 'Capital' and 'Labour': *Punch*; 'Tremendous Sacrifice!': Reproduced by permission of the Trustees of the British Museum

18 'Milling a Charley': Reproduced by permission of Thomas Nelson; 'Peeling a Charley': from D.G. Browne, *The Rise of Scotland Yard*, Harrap

19 poacher: Reproduced by courtesy of the Trustees of the British Museum; Peelers: Radio Times Hulton Picture Library; execution: Mansell Collection

20 Harrow: Guildhall Library, City of London; Whitechapel: Mansell Collection

21 board game: Museum of Childhood, Edinburgh

22 The Young Pretender: Reproduced by permission of the Trustees of the British Museum

23 Quebec: The National Maritime Museum, London

24 letter: Reproduced by permission of the Trustees of the British Museum

25 projected invasion: Mansell Collection; 'Wellington Boot': Victoria and Albert Museum, Crown copyright

26 plan: *The Manchester Observer*

27 consequences of voting against landlord: Mansell Collection; corruption at elections: Reproduced by courtesy of the Trustees of the British Museum

28 'British Beehive': Great Exhibition Reproduced by permission of the Trustees of the British Museum

29 bank holidays: *Illustrated London News*; 'Derby Day': Tate Gallery